Review of Scottis
D0505593

To Helena Mennie Shire, 1912–1991,
an outstanding and inspiring scholar,

and

to commemorate the opening of their
doors by Scottish Universities to women
students, in 1892

Review of Scottish Culture 8

Edited by
ALEXANDER FENTON
with
Hugh Cheape and Rosalind K Marshall

CANONGATE ACADEMIC
and
THE NATIONAL MUSEUMS OF SCOTLAND
EDINBURGH

Address for Reviews, Correspondence, etc:
Editors, ROSC, National Museums of Scotland,
Queen Street, Edinburgh EH2 1JD

Address for Subscriptions:
As above.

ROSC is published annually. Price £10 per issue.
Postage is extra.

Published with the financial aid of the Trustees of
The National Museums of Scotland
and of an anonymous donor.

Printed in Great Britain at the Alden Press, Oxford

Editorial Notes and Comments

This eighth issue of the **Review of Scottish Culture** involves both a dedication and a commemoration.

The dedication is to Helena Mennie Shire, an old friend who gave much inspiration to one of the Editors (AF) when he was a student at Cambridge. The Shire household was a kind of intellectual fermenting pot, where thoughts and ideas bubbled up from all sides, but where the visitor nevertheless felt completely at home. Whether for young students or more experienced scholars, the feeling was the same. Helena's contribution to literature and culture in general will have abiding value.

The commemoration is of the fact that in 1892, Scottish Universities first opened their doors to women students. To mark this year, the majority of the contributions to this issue are by women.

It is entirely coincidental but equally a source of pleasure that it was a woman who won the second Michaelis-Jena Ratcliff Prize (1992). She is Dr Anne O'Dowd, of the National Museum of Ireland, whose winning book, *Spalpeens and Tattie Hokers. History and Folklore of the Irish Migratory Agricultural Worker in Ireland and Britain*, is reviewed in this present volume. A special award was also made to the journal *Ulster Folklife*, for its outstanding contribution to ethnological studies. This prize, which is for studies in folklore or folklife relating to Britain and Ireland, is worth about £4000 annually and is now beginning to attract large numbers of entries. A prize of such value is an excellent means of stimulating ethnological studies and publications.

ROSC 8 maintains its customary wide sweep of all aspects of the culture of Scotland. In chronological terms the Norse mill at the Bu of Orphir in Orkney comes first. Though we do not as a rule include accounts of archaeological excavations (for which other journals are more appropriate), in this case we have made an exception because of the interest of the subject for the later history of horizontal mills. It is a function of ethnological studies to gather data that can narrow the parameters for the interpretation by archaeologists of the past; but this can also be a two-way process.

We have included two important transcripts of original source material in the Scottish Record Office. One is a gardener's diary relating to Orkney, 1801, kept by Hugh Ross, a native of Lochaber, whose English spelling on occasion betrays a Gaelic basis to his speech, and who includes one phrase in Gaelic that he thought too impolite for the language of the majority. The second is the detailed account of the sixteenth-century salmon fishings in Strathnaver.

A noteworthy feature also of this issue is the emphasis on oral history. Everyone has his or her own historical niche, involving a unique segment of history, and all can contribute to the general knowledge of the heritage. Gillian Munro, Margaret King and Dorothy Kidd exemplify how much valuable material can be rescued through systematic investigation.

Archaeology, gardening, music and painting, oral traditions, fishing, the history of the home and its plenishings, and games in the shape of curling stones meet and mingle in this volume, but the common theme remains that of the heritage.

Footnote

The Michaelis-Jena Ratcliff Prize The third award of the Michaelis-Jena Ratcliff Prize has been made to Dr Gabrielle Hatfield, BA Hons, for an important contribution, well-based on field research, on *Traditional Plant Remedies during the Twentieth Century in East Anglia*.

The number of entrants for the prize was high, and competition was strong. Because of the quality generally, a 'Highly Commended' award was initiated, and was made to Dr Cynthia Sughrue, BA, for her work on *Continuity, Conflict and Change: A Contextual and Comparative Study of Three South Yorkshire Longsword Dance Teams*.

The prize, currently standing at £4,000, is awarded annually. The final submission date (by publishers or by individuals) in each year is 31 December. For application forms and detailed Guidelines, contact John K Burleigh WS, Drummond Miller WS, 31/32 Moray Place, Edinburgh, EH3 6BZ.

Contributors

Colleen E. Batey, Art Gallery and Museum, Glasgow

A.D. Boney, formerly Professor of Botany, University of Glasgow

George Bruce, writer and broadcaster, Edinburgh

Annette Carruthers, Leverhulme Research Fellow, Edinburgh and St Andrews

Nancy Hewison, Kirkwall, Orkney

Dorothy I. Kidd, Scottish Ethnological Archive, National Museums of Scotland, Edinburgh

Margaret H. King, Arbroath Museum

Nicholas Mayhew, Heberden Coin Room, Ashmolean Museum of Art and Archaeology, Oxford

Jennifer Melville, Aberdeen Art Gallery and Museums

John Morrison, Miller, Garrabost, Lewis

Gillian Munro, Postgraduate Researcher, School of Scottish Studies, Edinburgh

Athol L. Murray, Former Keeper, Scottish Record Office, Edinburgh

David B. Smith, Sheriff of Kilmarnock

Evelyn Stell, Researcher, Department of Music, University of Glasgow

Contents

Page

1. Helena Mennie Shire, c. 1976.

Helena Mennie Shire
Aberdeen 1912–Cambridge 1991

Alisoun Gardner-Medwin

Helena Mary Mennie was born in Aberdeen, the daughter of John Mennie, headmaster, and his wife Jane Rae. She was educated at the High School, of which she became head girl, and at Aberdeen University, where she graduated *summa cum laude* in 1933. She then continued her studies at Cambridge, where she took a First in the English Tripos and started her career of literary research. In 1936 she married Edward Shire, Fellow of

2. At the back door of 98 Leslie Terrace, Aberdeen, in the 1920s. Left to right: Helena Mary Mennie (elder daughter), Jane E. Mennie (mother—née Rae), Elma Rae Mennie (younger daughter). By courtesy of Andrew Shire.

3. After a walk in the Aberdeenshire countryside, in the 1920s. Left to right: two teacher friends (names unknown), Helena Mary Mennie, John Mennie (father – headmaster in Aberdeen), Elma Rae Mennie. By courtesy of Andrew Shire.

King's College, Cambridge, a distinguished physicist.

Although her marriage meant that Helena Mennie Shire would thereafter make her home in Cambridge, she never forgot her native Scotland. Her research was centred on the poetry of Renaissance Scotland, yet was never insular, for her great strength lay in setting the culture of the Stewart courts within their politico-cultural relationships with other European courts, of England, France and Italy. This may be seen in her major work, *Song, Dance and Poetry of the Court of Scotland under King James VI* (1969), for which the research was supported by a Senior Research Fellowship of the Carnegie Trust. In this book she developed ideas first published in *Music of Scotland, 1500–1700. Musica Britannica XV* (1957), for which she edited the words of the songs, and in several shorter works such as 'The sweepings of Parnassus: Four Poems transcribed from the Record Books of the Burgh Sasines of Aberdeen' (1955) and the volumes of *The Ninth of May* series, *Poems from Panmure House* (1960), *Poems and Songs of Sir Robert Ayton* (1961) and *The Thrissil, The Rois and the Flour-de-lys: a sample book of state poems and love-songs showing affinities between Scotland, England and France in the sixteenth and seventeen centuries* (1962). Influence from England and France was also important for the poetry of *Alexander Montgomerie* (1960).

The *Montgomerie* book was published by the Saltire Society, for which she wrote other articles and gave lectures. Helena Mennie Shire was an enthusiastic member of the Saltire Society, serving for many years on the Council and as President of the Cambridge branch. From the 1940s onwards Helena Shire taught and lectured at Cambridge University, where she was a founding fellow of Robinson College. During the 1940s she taught English to men and women from Poland, and her friendship with the people of Poland lasted all her life, culminating in her trusteeship of the Corbridge Trust which encourages cultural exchanges between Poland and Britain. In 1991 she was awarded the Order of Merit of the Republic of Poland. She was also a prime mover in the *International Conferences on Scottish Language and Literature (Medieval and Renaissance)* where her ideas about international cultural relationships found an eager audience of scholars from all over the world.

During her last decade, Helena Mennie Shire lovingly researched the life and poetry of Olive Fraser, whom she had known when both were students, at Aberdeen and at Cambridge. *The Pure Account* (1981) and *The Wrong Music* (1989) made accessible the fine lyrics of a twentieth-century Scottish poet. It was the poetry of Scotland which was Helena Mennie Shire's great love, and perhaps that is why it gave her so much pleasure when, in 1988, Aberdeen University honoured her with the degree of LL.D.

Cauld blaws the Blast across the Moor, an early painting by John MacWhirter rediscovered

Jennifer Melville

The recent arrival of a small Victorian oil painting at Aberdeen Art Gallery prompted some raised eyebrows from the curatorial staff. The owner had presumed that the painting—a Scottish landscape—(Fig. 1) was by the well-known Victorian landscape artist, John MacWhirter RA HRSA RI (1838–1911). However, there were reasons to doubt this attribution. The painting depicted a Highland landscape with several figures battling through a storm. MacWhirter, a painter of the High Victorian era, is remembered particularly for his highly finished Claudian idylls such as *Morning—Isle of Arran 'All in the Blue, unclouded weather'* (Fig. 2). Compared with such paintings, this recent acquisition seemed totally at variance with the recognised style of the artist. Furthermore, the foreground was roughly worked, some areas being particularly weak. Although MacWhirter's paintings are not all of the highest standard, his work is generally of a high quality. The faulty technique of this painting therefore suggested a less talented hand.

Over a period of several weeks it was possible to establish that the painting was indeed by MacWhirter, but an example of his very early work. As such, it gives us an insight into this period of his life and illustrates the danger of categorising too strictly the paintings of a particular artist—certain features of MacWhirter's paintings were to change drastically during his long career. The painting also reveals the strong association which MacWhirter had with some of his contemporaries, especially with Peter Graham, and with the generation of Scottish artists which was to follow him. It was the influence of these associations which provided the key to understanding the painting which Aberdeen Art Gallery had newly acquired.

John MacWhirter was born at Slateford, near Edinburgh. His father was a paper manufacturer but, more importantly for his artistic son, also an amateur geologist and botanist who instilled a love of nature in John at an early age. MacWhirter was enrolled at the Trustees' Academy in Edinburgh in 1851, becoming a pupil of Scotland's foremost Drawing Master of the day, the highly influential Robert Scott Lauder. Lauder's pupils were to form what has been called the first truly Scottish School of painting, and MacWhirter's fellow students included such notable Victorian artists as William Quiller Orchardson (1833–1878), William McTaggart (1835–1910) and Peter Graham (1836–1921).

In 1864 MacWhirter followed in the path of most of Lauder's pupils by going to London. The following year he had a painting accepted at the Royal Scottish Academy. Although slower than some of his contemporaries, his ascent to the higher echelons of the established art world was steady. He was elected an associate member

1. *Cauld blaws the Blast across the Moor* by John MacWhirter. Measurements, 35.3 × 53.4 cm.

of the Royal Scottish Academy in 1867 and of the Royal Academy in 1879, becoming an honorary member of the Scottish Academy in 1882 and a full member of the Royal Academy in 1893.

Throughout his career MacWhirter travelled widely—to Norway and Italy and even as far as California—all the time furthering his knowledge and understanding of landscape painting. By 1869 he had settled in London, where he made a successful career painting imposing landscapes. His paintings display a great attention to detail. With Pre-Raphaelite precision each leaf and twig is delineated. Typically these expansive scenes are imbued with a Turneresque glow of warm and vibrant colours. Few figures inhabit these idylls. Instead the landscape itself, especially the trees (often graceful birch) are given anthropomorphic qualities. This successful formula, which appealed so much to Victorian taste, was usually completed with a poetic and rather long-winded title. This places these paintings definitely in the Late Victorian period—a time of melodrama and sentimentality. Most years the Royal Academy would display, to general acclaim, at least one such painting: in 1889 *Autumn 'With his gold hand gilting the falling leaf' (Chatterton)*; in 1898 the aforementioned *Morning—Isle of Arran 'All in the Blue, unclouded weather'*; and in 1899 *The silver strand, Loch Katrine 'So wondrous, wild, the whole might seem, the scenery of a fairy dream' (Lady of the Lake)*.

The bleak, forbidding scene, recently acquired for Aberdeen Art Gallery, could not have been further from these poetic and serene landscapes. Furthermore, closer examination of the painting revealed a dubious signature 'J. McWhirter' in the lower right-hand corner (Fig. 3). MacWhirter almost always signed his paintings 'MacW' (Fig. 4). In an exhibition of his work held in 1984,[1]

2. *Morning—Isle of Arran 'All in the Blue unclouded weather'* (formerly *Corrie, Isle of Arran*).

of over fifty paintings included, all without exception had the 'MacW' monogram[2]. Lastly, MacWhirter was also widely copied, which provided yet another reason to question the attribution.

The major difficulty with this suspicion was that the painting had an excellent provenance. It was part of the collection of Alexander Marr of 27 Carden Place, Aberdeen. He was the publisher of *The Aberdeen Free Press* (the forerunner of *The Press and Journal*). Marr died in 1917 aged 85, and his entire collection passed by descent to his great-grandson who donated this painting to Aberdeen Art Gallery. The collection, which included work by James Farquharson, Thomas Faed, Samuel Bough, Horatio McCulloch and John 'Spanish' Phillip, was probably acquired throughout the 1870s and 1880s. Marr did not employ a dealer and would have bought directly from exhibitions or from the artists. He was, therefore, unlikely to have been duped.

In spite of his popularity with the public, MacWhirter's work was not always greeted with universal acclaim. Caw, for example, whilst conceding that he was 'a charming colourist, occasionally producing effects of great delicacy', criticised MacWhirter's technique as weak.[3] In fact, the perfection of MacWhirter's painting formula was not achieved until the late 1880s, some twenty years after the beginning of his career. The weakness of execution of part of the painting was therefore not decisive as regards the attribution.

More problematic was the subject matter of the painting. Yet even this feature proved to be explicable. MacWhirter's early work was very similar in certain respects to the work of other Lauder pupils with whom he had remained friends even after his move to London. Often he would accompany a fellow-artist on a painting tour: he was with Orchardson in Heidelberg in 1860 and with Chalmers on Arran in September 1867. The contact amongst the group was very close.

When living in Edinburgh, MacWhirter met with his friends on a regular basis at the studios of George Paul Chalmers in Pitt Street. The young artists—Orchardson, Pettie, McTaggart, Chalmers and Cameron—held an informal painting class where a theme would be chosen for all to work on. These meetings continued throughout the late 1860s and 1870s when the artists moved to London. The close contact led to a similarity of subject matter and even of style. In landscape, evident in all their work at this time was a feeling of desolation and bleakness. The influence of man on the landscape was small, figures were few, and the landscape itself came to dominate. There was what has been called an 'increasing Victorian interest in the bleak and the misty'.[4] The weather (usually bad) also became as much a theme in the painting as the landscape.

MacWhirter clearly produced work of this genre, as early Royal Academy listings reveal: in 1873 he showed 'Desolate', in 1874 'Out in the Cold', and in 1875 'Land of the Mountain and the Flood'. It was therefore possible to explain the subject matter of Aberdeen's new painting on the assumption that it was a product of this early period of his life.

However, the problem of the signature remained. A study of the Royal Academy listings revealed that MacWhirter, at the outset of his long career, spelt his name 'McWhirter' and frequently signed his paintings 'J Mcwhirter'. 'Mac' and 'Mc' were interchangeable to a certain extent

3. *Cauld Blaws the Blast across the Moor* by John MacWhirter (detail of signature).

4. *Morning—Isle of Arran 'All in the Blue unclouded weather'* (detail of monogram).

in the nineteenth century when spelling, especially of names, was more free than it is today. Since his first year of exhibiting at the Royal Academy was in 1865, some eleven years after he first exhibited at the RSA, it can be assumed that MacWhirter produced numerous paintings in the intervening years signed in full with his name spelt in the earlier way. By 1868 he was still signing his name in full but had altered the spelling to MacWhirter. It appears thus on one of his most frequently illustrated paintings, *Night most Glorious Night, Thou wert not made for Slumber* (Royal Holloway College, University of London). Soon afterwards, as he became better known, he could abbreviate the signature to the familiar 'MacW', safe in the knowledge that the *cognoscenti* would recognise his distinctive monogram.

The conclusion that the newly acquired landscape was a genuine MacWhirter presented yet another problem, since it bore remarkable similarities to an as yet untraced painting by Joseph Farquharson RA (1846–1935) entitled *Cauld blaws the wind frae East tae West* (Fig. 5).[5] This painting was exhibited at the Royal Academy in 1880. The Farquharson appears to be an enlarged version of the right-hand side of the MacWhirter. In both paintings a mother guides her family through a stormy landscape. In the MacWhirter, sheltering one child under her arm, she turns to face the older child who struggles up the hilly path, clinging to his hat. The Farquharson differs only slightly. The mother, one child beside her, another now visible on her back wrapped in a shawl, is followed by the same child, again clinging to his hat. On the horizon a figure, probably the father, disappears into the distance. More attention is paid to the foreground in the Farquharson, the distant hills only suggested. MacWhirter gives the landscape more prominence—the figures are somewhat peripheral—but otherwise the two paintings bear remarkable similarities.

John MacWhirter and Joseph Farquharson have often been said to represent two quite different sides of the Scottish landscape. Whilst Farquharson concentrated on

5. *Cauld blaws the Wind frae East tae West* by Joseph Farquharson.

the bleak, cold, snow-clad hills of winter, MacWhirter normally showed a sunny, light-filled scene. Yet these two paintings, which resembled each other so closely, seemed unlike the recognised work of either artist.

Farquharson was too young to have been taught by Lauder and was not included in the informal artistic gatherings of Lauder's pupils. He was, however, a pupil of Peter Graham, who was one of the artists who had studied under Lauder and who was one of the friends with whom MacWhirter had often worked. Through Graham, Farquharson came into close contact with the 'Lauder School'. He was particularly close to G.P. Chalmers, travelling to the Netherlands with him in 1874 and entertaining him at his Finzean home the same year.

Although few of Farquharson's earliest paintings have been traced, Sir George Reid PRSA reveals their artistic genealogy when commenting on those exhibited at the RSA in 1867, saying that they 'have much of Peter Graham about them but good and full of promise'.[6] The interesting feature of Graham's paintings is that they were the bleak Scottish landscapes already detailed. It is precisely for such paintings that he is remembered!

The year 1880, when his *Cauld blaws the Wind frae East tae West* was exhibited, was a watershed for Farquharson, for this was when he began to study under Carolus-Duran in Paris. Under the tutelage of Carolus-Duran and by mixing with artists such as John Singer Sargent, Farquharson's style became grander and his canvases more expansive. He moved away from the earlier influences of Lauder's pupils.

As in the case of MacWhirter, there is a tendency today to remember the later paintings of Joseph Farquharson (specifically the snowscapes), which brought him such international success. In his early years, however, Farquharson's snow scenes were a rarity. Rather, it is clear that in the 1870s his output was often very similar in character to that of MacWhirter due to the influence of the Lauder school on both of them. It is interesting to observe that in 1870 MacWhirter exhibited at the RSA a painting with a remarkably similar title to the untraced Farquharson: *Cauld blaws the Blast across the Moor*. It seems likely that this is the painting now acquired for Aberdeen Art Gallery.

A painting which at first sight was of questionable authenticity has turned out to be a very exciting find. It enhances our understanding of MacWhirter's early career and illustrates his continuity with the generation of Scottish artists who followed him. The influence of the Lauder school on both MacWhirter and Farquharson suggests the important conclusion that we have found the painting first exhibited by MacWhirter at the Royal Scottish Academy in 1870.

Notes

1. Malcolm Innes Gallery, Edinburgh.
2. Malcolm Innes Gallery Exhibition Catalogue, 'John MacWhirter' by Malcolm Innes and Anthony Wood 1984 (p.4).
3. James L. Caw, *Scottish Painting, 1620–1908* Kingsmead 1908, 257.
4. David and Francina Irwin, *Scottish Painters at Home and Abroad, 1700–1900* Faber and Faber 1975, 357. Another was sold at Sotheby's (Glasgow), 5 February 1991 (26).
5. The photograph of this untraced painting is in the possession of the Farquharson family. A reduced version of the painting was exhibited in 'Joseph Farquharson of Finzean', Aberdeen Art Gallery 1985 (40).
6. Aberdeen Art Gallery Exhibition Catalogue, 'Joseph Farquharson of Finzean', by Francina Irwin, 1985, 6.

Other sources not listed in the notes

(a) W. Hardie, Scottish Painting 1837 to the present, in *Studio Vista* (1990).

(b) E. Pinnington, *George Paul Chalmers RSA and the art of his time*, Annan & Sons 1896.

(c) Dr. L. Errington, *Master Class—Robert Scott Lauder and his Pupils*, National Galleries of Scotland 1983.

I am indebted to Francina Irwin and the late Sheenah Smith for their help with this article.

Lady Jean Campbell's Seventeenth-Century Music-Book

Evelyn Stell

Introduction

In 1645 Lady Jean Campbell, elder daughter of the Earl of Loudoun, in Ayrshire, married George Maule, heir to the sizeable Panmure estate in Angus. Among the books which she took with her on her journey across Scotland was a small vellum-bound manuscript bearing her name and containing music which she had played on lute and harpsichord as a young girl in Loudoun Castle. This book, as MS 9449, now forms part of the Panmure Collection of music manuscripts deposited in the National Library of Scotland.

The Panmure Collection[1] was purchased by the Library in 1957 and 1979, and contains thirty music manuscripts of British and Continental provenance, ranging in date from the late sixteenth to the early nineteenth centuries. The seventeenth-century volumes are especially important. Duncan Burnett's Music-book[2] contains keyboard pieces of high quality by William Kinloch and by Burnett himself, who is known to have run the Glasgow song-school in the 1630s.[3] Clement Matchett's Virginal Book[4] is of English origin, and a valuable source of the music of the Elizabethan virginal school, including works by William Byrd and John Bull. Two volumes of lute music contain over 100 lute pieces by contemporary French composers of note, such as the Gaultier family, Pinel and Mesangeau.[5] One of these lute manuscripts is believed to be in Mesangeau's own hand.

Compared to these sources, Lady Jean Campbell's Music-book has tended to be dismissed as being of an inferior standard (see below p.15 and note 19). Whether or not this criticism is valid, this manuscript deserves to be judged on different terms: its owner's status as the possible originator of the entire Panmure musical tradition gives her book a wider historical importance, and the manuscript itself appears to represent a comparatively rare survival in Scotland of a volume known to have been used by a young lady as part of her musical education.

The Manuscript

The manuscript is an oblong octavo volume measuring 18.4 cm by 14.4 cm. Although it has been rebound by the Library, its original vellum binding has been left visible, bearing the emblem and initials ('IC') of its owner. The manuscript contains seventy-five folios, originally unnumbered:

> f[olio] 1r[ecto] contains an inscription, 'This booke are[?] / Ladie Jeane Campbell', and some heavily obliterated words;
>
> ff.3r–10v[erso] contain eight keyboard pieces;
>
> ff.10v–43r contain forty-six pieces in lute tablature; and
>
> f.75v contains the possibly significant names:
>
> 'M. Moner'; 'Monsieur Dozell'.

The book otherwise consists of blank

pages, with occasional jottings, including some poetry.

Dating the manuscript is difficult. Given that there is no indication that the volume was ever used reversed (that is, turned upside down, and started again from the rear, a common seventeenth-century practice), the eight keyboard pieces can be taken to be the earliest portion of the manuscript. Judging from the uniformity of ink and script, they appear to have been copied, very neatly, by one person at one time. That the copyist was Lady Jean herself is indicated by the initials 'IC' after the titles of pieces 1 and 3 and at the end of the final piece. The careful and deliberate script suggests that the writer of this part of the manuscript was a young girl copying under instruction.

Some of the jottings may provide clues to a more precise dating of this early portion. On f.1 two lines of writing are quite deliberately and thoroughly scribbled over. On the first of the obscured lines three words have been crossed out: the last two of these are definitely 'Jeane Campbell', while the first word, much more difficult to decipher, looks like 'Mistres'. These are written in the same hand which copied the keyboard pieces, presumably that of Lady Jean. The hand which made the correction is in a quite different style, but could be Lady Jean's at a later age.

Sir John Campbell was created Earl of Loudoun in 1633,[6] but for political reasons the title was withheld until 1641. It is likely that it was around this time that the change of style of his elder daughter from 'Mistress' to 'Lady' was effected, and it therefore seems reasonable to conclude that the flyleaf inscription was corrected in or after 1641, and that the keyboard pieces had been copied before that date. The styles of these eight keyboard pieces correspond comfortably with a *c.*1630–1640 copying date. Six are dances or masque pieces in the style of the first half of the seventeenth century. Of the remaining two, one seems to be a folk tune, the other a study in an earlier keyboard style.

Precisely when Jean Campbell was born, following her parents' marriage in 1620[7] is unknown. She herself married in 1645 when, an eligible young lady, she may have been about nineteen or twenty years of age. A date of birth of *c.*1625 would have made her about fourteen or fifteen when she compiled the keyboard part of the manuscript, probably under a teacher's instruction, in *c.*1640, and fifteen or sixteen when she became 'Lady' Jean Campbell in 1641. The maturity of the script and the technical ability required to play the pieces would support this suggested chronology.

The portion of the manuscript devoted to lute tablature is even less easy to date. Two hands are involved, both of which seem more professional than that of a pupil copying under instruction; it is likely that they represent two teachers of the lute, although the talented Lady Jean herself cannot be ruled out entirely. The music itself is entirely of the French school of lute music led by Ennemond Gaultier which was very popular in seventeenth-century Britain, and the tunings used (see below) point to the middle of the century. There is even a possibility that the writers are French, conceivably the 'M. Moner' and 'Monsieur Dozell', otherwise unidentified, whose scribbled names appear on f.75v.

Historical Background—The Campbells of Loudoun

Sir John Campbell of Lawers (1598–1663), Jean's father, married Margaret, Baroness of Loudoun, in 1620 and acquired the Ayrshire barony in his wife's right in 1622.[8] He was created Earl of Loudoun in 1633 but, a staunch Covenanter, he opposed the king's policies in the same year, and the title was suspended. In 1641, however, he was appointed Lord High Chancellor of Scotland and First Commissioner of the Treasury, and at the same time was allowed to resume his earldom.[9] He had four children, two boys and two girls, Jean being his elder daughter. As argued above, she was born probably in about 1625.

In the years before her marriage in 1645, Jean Campbell's family enjoyed great prosperity. The earl made extensive additions to his principal residence, Loudoun Castle, and redeveloped Loudoun Hall, his town house in Ayr.[10] Like any other girl in her position, Jean would have received a thorough grounding in domestic concerns, and tuition in social accomplishments, with a high-ranking marriage as the goal.

Music was one of the more important of these accomplishments, and the lute and the virginal—the two instruments for which Jean's book was written—were the most popular choices for young ladies to learn to play. To judge from her subsequent history and from the quality and standard of difficulty of the other keyboard manuscripts in the Panmure Collection, she seems to have developed a real interest in music for its own sake, and to have become a performer of considerable skill.

Generally, young ladies in the seventeenth century would receive their music lessons at home. If tuition was required to a standard not available locally, however, the pupil might have to spend some time in one of the larger towns. There is circumstantial evidence to suggest that one of Jean Campbell's keyboard teachers was Duncan Burnett, whose music-book is also part of the Panmure Collection. This tuition could have taken place in the early 1640s, when Burnett, whether or not still in charge of the song school, was almost certainly living in Glasgow, where he died in 1651.[11] Some jottings on the Burnett manuscript could be interpreted as evidence that Duncan Burnett did indeed give instruction to the daughters of the nobility. Two names are recorded: 'Issobel Mowatt' and 'Lucie Hamilton', who adds to her signature the words, 'good lord have marcie upon me', a weary scribble suggesting that not all young ladies were enthusiastic about their practising. According to Kenneth Elliott, this was very likely to have been Lucie Hamilton of the Abercorn branch of the family, whose projected marriage fell through in 1627 and who died single sometime after 1688.[12] Lucie must have been older than Jean Campbell, and her use of the book would have taken place before Jean could have acquired it, and perhaps also the Matchett manuscript, from her teacher.

Historical Background—The Maules of Panmure[13]

The ancestry of the Maule family in Britain can be traced back to the time of the Norman Conquest; in Scotland they came to prominence in the thirteenth century, after about 1224, when they acquired the considerable Panmure lands in Angus. They continued to gain in wealth and standing, and their support of the Crown was rewarded in 1646 when Patrick Maule was created Earl of Panmure by Charles I. A year earlier, in 1645, his eldest son, George, had married Lady Jean Campbell.

Although political motives were no doubt significant in its arrangement, the marriage seems to have been a very happy one. The next few years were certainly eventful for Lady Jean. Her husband was an active Royalist in the Civil War: as colonel of the Forfarshire Horse, he took part in the Battle of Dunbar in September 1650 and was wounded at Inverkeithing in July 1651. He took little further part in public matters under the Protectorate, but the Restoration in 1660 created a more favourable political climate for the Maules. In 1661, on the death of his father, George became 2nd Earl of Panmure, and he and Lady Jean, now Countess of Panmure, embarked on an ambitious plan to create a new and

1. Panmure House, Angus, prior to its demolition in 1955 (Crown copyright, Royal Commission on the Ancient and Historical Monuments of Scotland).

splendid family seat[14] (Fig. 1) which was not completed until after the Earl's death in 1671. George, the eldest of their three sons, succeeded as 3rd Earl but died in 1686 without an heir. His brother James became 4th Earl.

Lady Jean herself survived until about 1703 and was probably interred in the family mausoleum attached to the church at Panbride, near Carnoustie. The mausoleum was created by her son George in 1681, and remains the only extant piece of seventeenth-century architecture of the Maule family.[15]

The Jacobite sympathies of James, 4th Earl of Panmure, and his involvement in the Rebellion of 1715, led to a temporary eclipse of the family fortunes when the Panmure estates were forfeited in the following year. On his death in 1723 James was succeeded by his brother Harry, who was known simply as Mr Harry Maule of Kellie, a neighbouring barony. Harry died in 1734, and his son, William, was eventually able to purchase back the Panmure estates in 1764. William's sister, Jean, had married the son of the 6th Earl of Dalhousie, and through this connection the Panmure inheritance ultimately came to the Dalhousie family, from whom the manuscripts were purchased by the National Library of Scotland.

The number and variety of the surviving manuscripts suggest that the Panmure household had a much greater than normal enjoyment of music in the seventeenth and eighteenth centuries, and the beginnings of this intense musical activity do seem to have coincided with Lady Jean Campbell's arrival in the family. James and Harry, Lady Jean's sons, made several cultural tours abroad, during which they doubtless collected most of the continental manuscripts. After the forfeiture in 1716 James spent time in Italy, and the score of an Italian opera, 'Anagilda', is dated 8 March 1717, at Pesaro (MSS 9470-2). Harry was evidently a performer on the viola da gamba, his signature appearing on the flyleaf of the bass part of a set of viol part-books (MSS 9455–7). In the Panmure Collection there are also several other substantial French manuscripts for viol dating from the latter part of the seventeenth century. Two manuscripts of violin music, and the fact that the first violin part of 'Anagilda' was also brought from Italy, suggest that a member of the family, possibly James, was a violinist.

There were probably plenty of opportunities for music-making at Panmure in the lifetime of Lady Jean Campbell. The survival of music part-books for up to five players implies that the gatherings were fairly large, involving friends as well as family. These would certainly have included the antiquarian, Robert Edward, minister of the neighbouring parish of Murroes, whose own Commonplace Book forms part of the Panmure Collection.[16]

The Keyboard Music

The harpsichord and the virginal were the principal keyboard instruments of the seventeenth century. Both were plucked stringed instruments operated by jacks and quills. The harpsichord was the larger, with greater length of string and resonance of sound, and was usually wing-shaped, the strings running away from the player, at right angles to the keyboard. It could have more than one manual and was often fitted with devices to change the register or even add a percussive effect. Duncan Burnett's Music-book includes a late sixteenth-century piece by William Kinloch which can be played only on a two-manual instrument.[17]

The virginal was smaller, more compact, and perhaps more suitable for a domestic environment. It was box-shaped, with the strings running across in front of the player, parallel to the keyboard. The keyboard itself was sometimes projecting, sometimes inset. It could be centrally placed or offset to left or right and its position affected the tone of the instrument.

The terms 'virginal' and 'harpsichord' were interchangeable and were sometimes referred to in the plural, as 'a pair of' harpsichords or virginals. The main source of supply for the Scottish nobility seems to have been England. In 1677, for example, we find Sir Hugh Campbell of an Argyll branch of the family writing about his daughter to his Edinburgh agent:

> . . . Iff I find Maggie ane extraordinar player on the virginellis she sall have an pair of the best harpsecordis that Ingland can afford, and therfor lett hir tak much panis . . .[18]

Lady Jean Campbell's Music-book affords no clue to the type of instrument she used, although the two-manual Kinloch piece in the Burnett book (which may have belonged to her) is playable only on a harpsichord.

Of the eight keyboard pieces themselves, Thurston Dart has commented:[19]

> In style these pieces belong to the period 1625–40, and it is rather sad to see from this manuscript, as from several others of the time, how sudden and how complete was the decay of the virginal school during these years . . . If the last two pieces of Lady Jean Campbell's book are, in fact, by Orlando Gibbons, they add no lustre to his reputation. Neither of these nor any other of the pieces in the book is at all outstanding, and the keyboard part of this manuscript has little to offer either the musician or the scholar.

Thus he dismisses the keyboard section of Lady Jean Campbell's book. Yet though the pieces do not compare in quality with the older Burnett and Matchett manuscripts, they have a musical value insofar as they demonstrate a process of transformation (rather than 'decay') undergone by British music in the period between the golden English Elizabethan age and the Restoration style of Blow, Locke and Purcell.

After the death of Gibbons in 1625, and with the notable exception of Thomas Tomkins (1573–1656), the virtuoso writing characteristic of the Elizabethan school of virginalists ceased, and the emphasis instead fell on the instrument's ability to accompany melodies, usually in chordal style—a trait perhaps foreshadowing the continuo rôle of keyboard instruments in the eighteenth century.

General changes in harmony are also particularly reflected in the Lady Jean keyboard pieces. The fluid harmonies which sixteenth-century composers inherited from medieval modality were hardening into the more definite major and minor key system of the Baroque period and later. In 1640 this change was only beginning, and the result can often be a 'wandering' tonality, with unconvincing modulations.

The pieces themselves include at least one, and probably five, masque tunes. The masque was a very popular form of dramatic entertainment in the first half of the seventeenth century in England, and was the direct precursor of English opera. Lavish and elaborate in concept, masques were spectacular displays including music, mime, dancing, costume and scenery. The music could take the form of songs, dances, or background music to tableaux and mime. Many of these items became well known in their own right, and are frequently found adapted for keyboard in contemporary manuscripts.[20] The four 'Almaynes' in this manuscript probably fall into this category. More is known about the piece entitled 'The Bears Daunce' (Figs. 2 and 3), which turns out to have been just that! Three performing bears danced to this lumbering tune in 1622, as part of Ben Jonson's masque, *Augurs*, the music of which is attributed to Alphonso Ferrabosco and Nicholas Lanier.[21]

The three remaining pieces consist of an untitled and as yet unidentified folksong-like melody, and two pieces, 'Ane Air' and 'Saraband', attributed to 'Orlando'. This is presumably Orlando Gibbons, but on stylistic grounds the attributions are almost certainly mistaken. Both pieces appear in other sources, one of which attributes the 'Saraband' to Richard Portman (d. *c.*1655), a pupil of Gibbons and better known as a composer of liturgical and organ music.[22]

The Lute Music

In the seventeenth century the lute continued to enjoy great popularity due to its self-sufficiency, its subtle power of expression and especially its elegance. It was a very fashionable instrument for young ladies to be taught, and one English teaching volume points out that '. . . for the advantages of marriage, how many bachelors and maids have we seen advanced by this agreeing harmony . . .'.[23] For all its social acceptability and charms, however, the instrument was not an easy one to play, besides being fragile and requiring constant tuning.

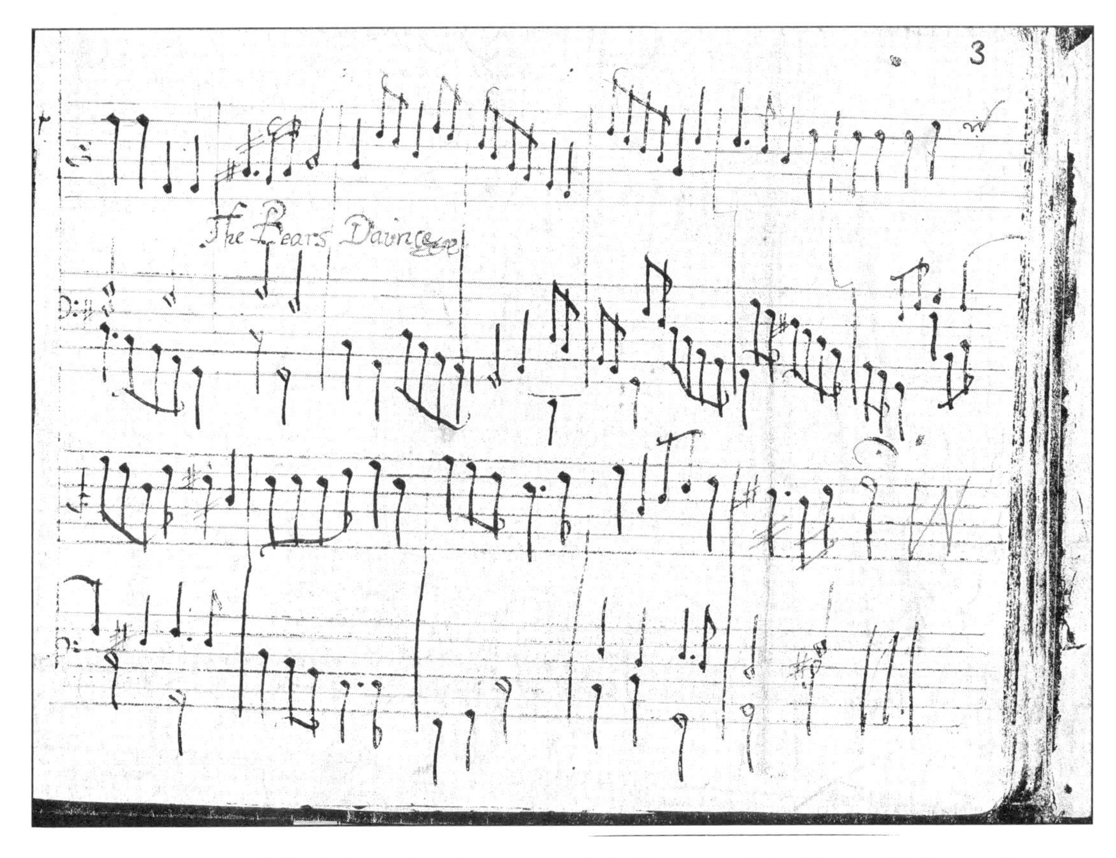

2. 'The Bears Daunce' (f.3r) (reproduced courtesy of the Trustees of the National Library of Scotland).

The lute's distinguishing features are its vaulted back, its bent-back pegbox, its preference for double strings or 'courses', and the surprising resonance of such a light and delicate instrument. The sixteenth-century lute possessed six courses, but later in the century some lutes acquired an additional lower course. This part of the instrument's register became the focus of the important changes which took place in the seventeenth century and which produced the instrument of the type played by Lady Jean Campbell. This had six bass courses or diapasons in addition to the original six: these were struck open (i.e. unstopped) and made greater use of the bass resonances of the instrument.

For several decades a number of different tunings were in evidence, until the 'D minor tuning', A–D–f–a–d–f′, became established in the last quarter of the century. The lute music in Lady Jean's manuscript uses two of the earlier Baroque tunings. She may well have owned more than one lute, in order to avoid too much re-tuning.

The notation is the French form of lute tablature, which was used in Britain in the seventeenth century. Six lines represent the lute's strings, letters on the lines indicate the frets on the fingerboard, and rhythm signs above the lines give an idea of note values. The bass courses are indicated by the letter 'a' below the stave. Oblique lines indicate which of the diapasons is to be used.

The forty-six lute pieces in this manuscript are written in the *style brisé*, a graceful contemporary French style in which broken chords and fragmented melodies use the resonance of the instrument to rich effect.

The pieces are mainly dance movements: allemandes, sarabandes and courantes. Only one composer is named, 'Goutier' (Gaultier), but two others have so far been identified, Mesangeau and Dufaut.[24]

The lutenist Ennemond Gaultier was the best known of a group of French lute composers whose music was copied and circulated widely in Britain as well as France. He was reported to have been greatly fêted by the English court on a visit there, probably in about 1630. The attribution of the 'Gaultier' piece in Lady Jean's book is, however, doubtful.[25] The Mesangeau piece, an allemande, is found in the first part of the lute section of the manuscript. Mesangeau, who died in 1638, was one of the earliest of this group of composers, and is believed to have been a teacher of Gaultier. The piece is attributed to Mesangeau in other, French, sources.[26] Dufaut was a later *style brisé* composer who died in the 1680s. The two identified pieces are in the latter portion of the lute music, and both are also found in French sources.[27]

Conclusions

The general mix and standard of the keyboard and lute pieces in this manuscript, the personal nature of the volume and the internal dating evidence cited above all point to Lady Jean Campbell's Music-book being used by a young lady of the aristocracy who, though not a beginner, is still at a learning stage. The book therefore has, in addition to its musical interest, a social significance rarely manifested elsewhere.

3. 'The Bears Daunce'; transcribed and edited by Evelyn Stell.

The closest known Scottish comparison is one of two seventeenth-century manuscripts discovered in 1979 among the Sutherland Papers; dated 1643, it belonged to Margaret Wemyss, whose sister later became Countess of Sutherland.[28] The content of this important manuscript is similar in many respects to that of Lady Jean's book, although greater in quantity. Its orthography and script, however, testify very obviously to the common neglect of basic literacy in the education of daughters of the nobility in the seventeenth century.[29]

Lady Jean Campbell's book, on the other hand, is characterised by an elegant script and a neatness and legibility of words and music. The evidence, adduced above, that she became an accomplished musician, and that she founded the remarkable Panmure musical tradition which led to such a treasure-house of music manuscripts, also gives her and her book a special place in the history of Scottish music.

I should like to make special acknowledgment of the help and guidance given to me by Dr Kenneth Elliott, Department of Music, University of Glasgow, who is supervising my research into the sources of seventeenth-century Scottish instrumental music.

Notes

1. N(ational) L(ibrary) (of) S(cotland), Catalogue of Manuscripts, MSS 9447–9476, Panmure House Music Books; Kenneth Elliott, Music of Scotland 1500–1700 (Unpublished Ph.D dissertation, University of Cambridge, 1960), *passim*; Patrick Cadell, The Panmure Music Manuscripts (Unpublished text of a lecture given to the Edinburgh Bibliographical Society on 25 October 1979). See also NLS, *Musica Scotica* (1957; catalogue of an exhibition of Scottish Music Books 1500–1700).
2. H. M. Willsher, 'An Early Scottish Virginal Book', *Scottish Historical Review*, xxxi (1952), 131–6; Thurston Dart, 'New Sources of Virginal Music', *Music and Letters*, xxxv (1954), 93–106; Kenneth Elliott, *Early Scottish Keyboard Music* (1958; revised edn., 1967); Kenneth Elliott and Frederick Rimmer, *A History of Scottish Music* (1973), 38–40, 44.
3. Scottish Burgh Records Society, *Extracts from the Records of the Burgh of Glasgow*, i, 1573–1642 (1876), 388.
4. Thurston Dart, ed., *Clement Matchett's Virginal Book (1612)* (1957, revised edn. 1969).
5. Andre Souris and Monique Rollin, eds., *Oeuvres de Belleville, Bouvier, Chancy, Chevalier et Du Buisson* (1967); *Oeuvres de Dufaut* (1965); *Oeuvres du Vieux Gaultier* (1966); *Oeuvres de Mesangeau* (1971); Monique Rollin and G. Vaccaro, eds., *Oeuvres de Dubut* (1979); *Oeuvres de Pinel* (1982), *passim.* See also Stanley Sadie, ed., *The New Grove Dictionary of Music and Musicians* (1980), *passim.*
6. Sir J. Balfour Paul, *The Scots Peerage* (1904–14), v, 506.
7. *Ibid.*
8. *Ibid.*, 506–7.
9. David Stevenson, *The Scottish Revolution, 1637–1644* (1973), 235–7.
10. A.H. Millar, *The Castles and Mansions of Ayrshire* (1885), 'Loudoun Castle'; David MacGibbon and Thomas Ross, *The Castellated and Domestic Architecture of Scotland*, v (1892), 321–5.
11. S(cottish) R(ecord) O(ffice), Commissary Courts Records, CC/9/7/31 (see *Glasgow Testaments*, 77).
12. Elliott, Music of Scotland, 353; *Scots Peerage*, i, 48; George Hamilton, *A History of the House of Hamilton* (1933), 36.
13. Except where otherwise stated, this section is based on information derived from J. Stuart, ed., *Registrum de Panmure* (1874), i, and *Scots Peerage*, vii.
14. R.S. Milne, *The Master Masons to the Crown of Scotland* (1893), 153–8, 232. Panmure House was demolished in 1955.
15. I should like to thank Reverend J. E. Stewart Low, minister of Panbride, for access and information concerning this church.
16. Helena M. Shire, 'Robert Edward's Commonplace Book and Scots Literary Tradition', and Kenneth Elliott, 'Robert Edward's Commonplace Book and Scots Musical History', *Scottish Studies*, v, (1961), 43–56; Kenneth Elliott and Helena M. Shire, *Music of Scotland 1500–1700 (Musica Britannica*, xv, 1957), *passim.*
17. Elliott, *Keyboard Music*, 17, 'Kinloche his Fantassie'.
18. *The Book of the Thanes of Cawdor* (1859), 338, cited by Rosalind K. Marshall, *Virgins and Viragos* (1983), 130. I should like to

thank Dr Marshall for general advice on the seventeenth-century social background.

19. Dart, 'New Sources', 100.
20. Howard Ferguson, ed., *Anne Cromwell's Virginal Book, 1638* (1974); Charles J. F. Cofone, ed., *Elizabeth Rogers' Virginal Book* (1975).
21. Andrew J. Sabol, *Songs and Dances for the Stuart Masques* (1959), 3, 120 (no. 42) and 172.
22. Gerald Hendrie, ed., *Orlando Gibbons' Keyboard Music (Musica Britannica*, xx (1967)), 103; Peter Le Huray, in *New Grove Dictionary*, xv, 138.
23. Thurston Dart, 'Miss Mary Burwell's Instruction Book for the Lute', *The Galpin Society Journal*, xi (1958), 49.
24. Souris and Rollin, *op. cit.*, n.5 above.
25. Souris and Rollin, *Gaultier*, xvii.
26. Souris and Rollin, *Mesangeau*, 37 (no. 34).
27. Souris and Rollin, *Dufaut*, 9 and 32 (nos 7 and 28).
28. NLS Dep. 314/23–4, Wemyss Music MSS. See also Matthew Spring, 'The Lady Margaret Wemyss Manuscript', *The Lute*, xxvii (1987), 5–29.
29. Marshall, *Virgins and Viragos*, 127.

A Norse Horizontal Mill in Orkney

Colleen E. Batey

The site known as the Earl's Bu, at Orphir on the North side of Scapa Flow, includes the remains of the Round Church and the adjacent Norse 'Hall', so often equated with references in the *Orkneyinga Saga* under the year 1135.[1] The church itself is fragmentary, having been partially removed during building of a later Parish Church immediately to its West; ironically, that church has subsequently been re-sited, and the structure itself removed. The other visible structural remains, uncovered in the 1930s, are difficult to interpret because they appear to be an amalgam of different structural phases, although it is presumed that they date from sometime in the Late Norse period (i.e. 11th–15th centuries).

In 1978, during a visit to the site by archaeologists who were then working at Birsay in the NW Mainland of Orkney, attention was drawn by the farmer, Mr Stephenson, to a feature which he had discovered several years previously. This feature was located by Mr Stephenson when he was preparing foundations for a barn (subsequently re-sited to the West) and was of a drystone 'tunnel-like' construction, with slab lintels and clay cappings. Initial investigation was restricted to recording the structure already revealed; in following years more extensive work was undertaken along the line of this 'tunnel-like' feature. It was considered most likely that the feature was part of a souterrain, an underground passage-chamber structure of a type located at other sites in Orkney, such as Grain or Rennibister,[2] and as commonly found in many areas of Scotland, dated to the early to mid First Millenium AD. This identification remained in place until 1989.

Sealing the line of the lintel slabs at the East end (the area originally exposed) was a clay bank, but this was replaced to the West by very extensive, rich and deep midden banks, dated within the earlier part of the Late Norse period (*c* 11th–12th Century). This material appears at least in part to have been dumped from the South, where the Norse buildings

1 Norse Horizontal Mill under excavation, from East. Photo P. G. Johnson.

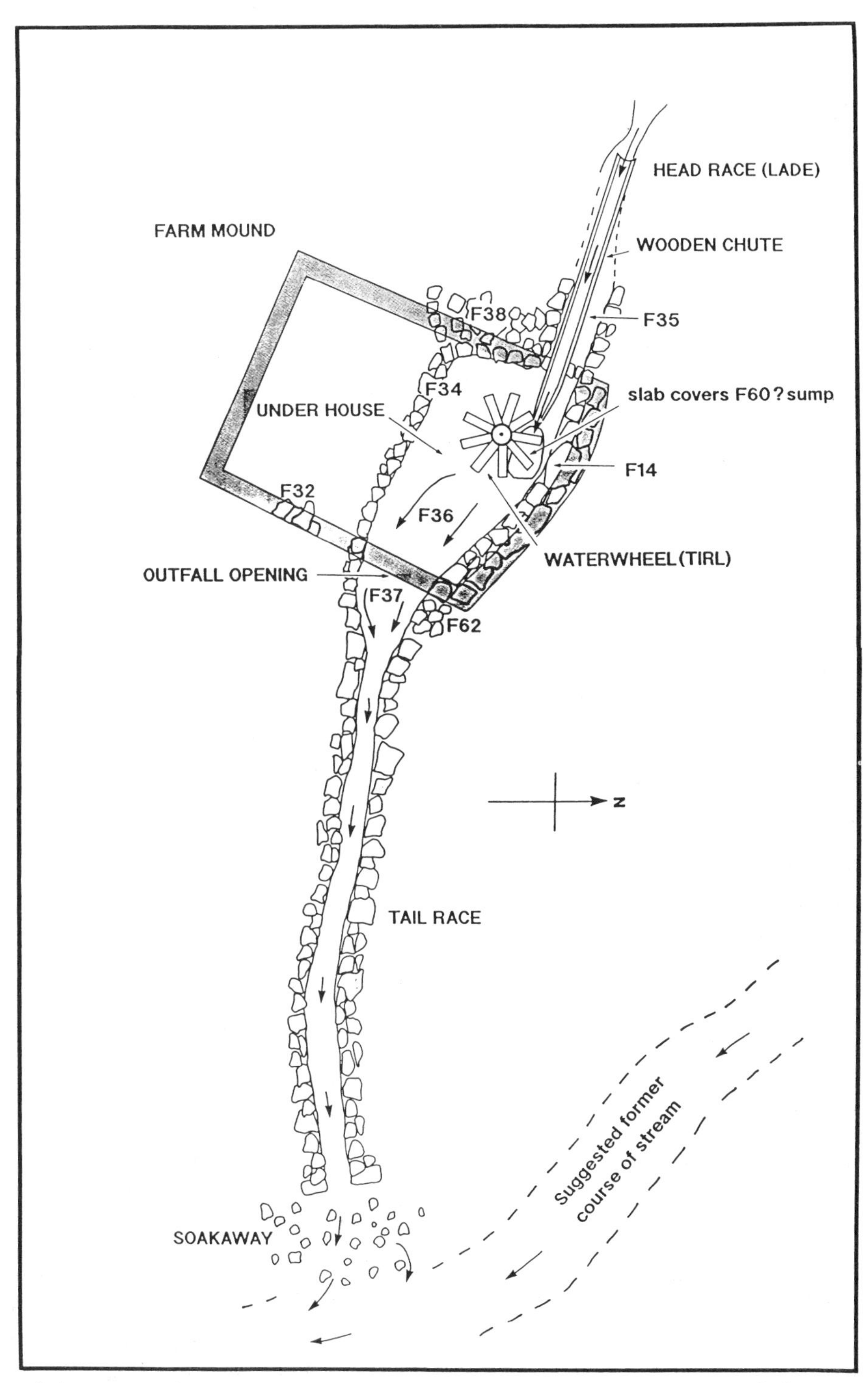

2. Plan of the excavated remains with additional elements added for reconstruction. Drawn by L. McEwan after M. Edgeworth.

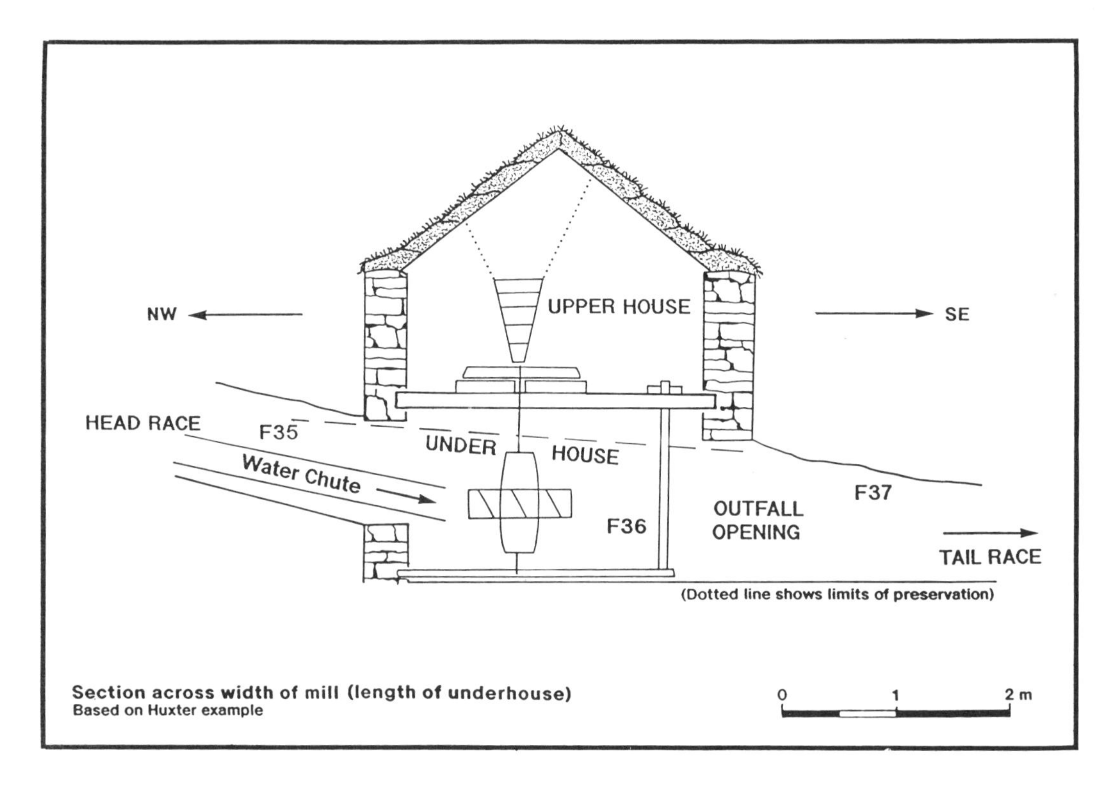

3. Suggested reconstruction in section across width of mill. Drawn by L. McEwan after M. Edgeworth.

of the Bu, or Earl's farm, have been located (see above). Some 10m to the West, dense middens formed the infill for a chamber-like expansion.

Investigation began to make it clear that the chamber at this end of the stone passage might have served a function not as a souterrain, but rather as an underhouse of a horizontal mill, seen here in excavation (see Fig.1). I am particularly grateful here for the work undertaken by Matthew Edgeworth and Paul Johnson on this aspect. They found it hard to persuade me that they were correct. The accompanying illustrations (Figs. 2–4) indicate the elements of this structure which have now been revealed. The underhouse which survives to over 1m is indicated by walls F14 to the North, F34 to the South, and F38 to the West. Possibly F32 to the East may represent a fragment of the upperhouse, but otherwise that part of the structure is missing. The lade or head race is identified with F35, a narrow chute-like feature with substantial slabs lying on end and with a slight gradient towards the underhouse. Later examples of this type of mill often have a wooden chute here. A small pond to allow a build-up of water pressure may also have been identified to the West, and the stone-covered leat or tail race (F37) leads away to the East, towards the burn. This latter feature was the original stone 'tunnel' examined in 1978.

Within the underhouse itself, there are traces of a small clay-lined depression located on the line of the lade (F60). It was thought that this must have been the position of the driveshaft for the wheel itself—although this would be unusual, since the driveshaft would not normally make contact with the ground, but rather be supported on a cross-piece or sole-tree. It is, however, interesting to note

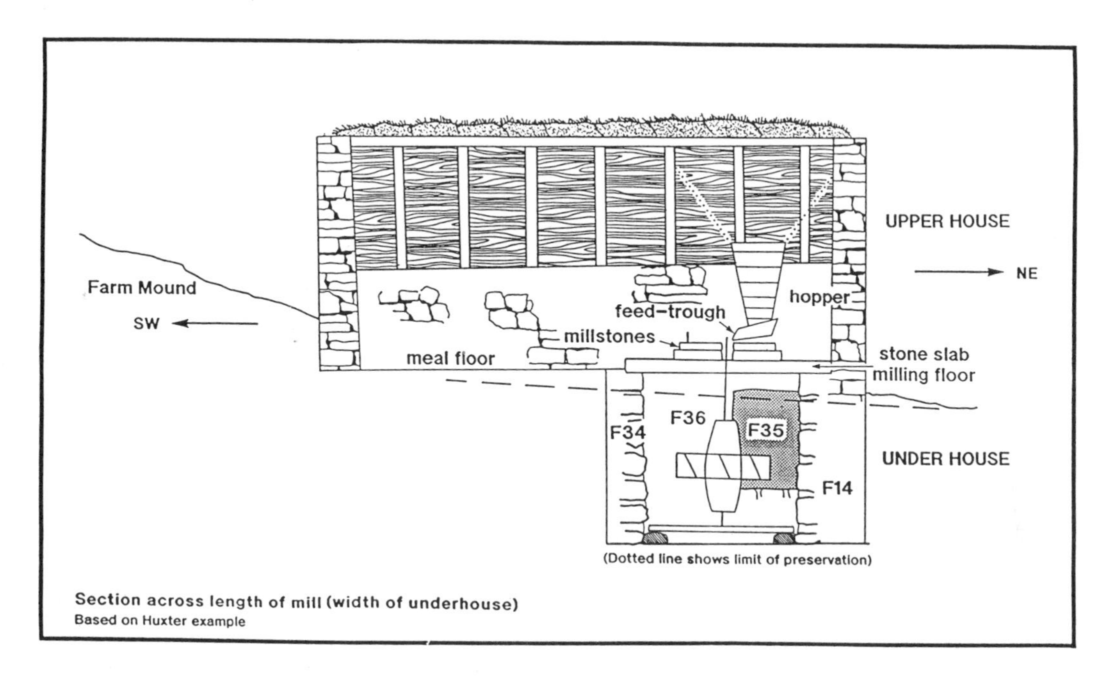

4. Suggested reconstruction in section across length of mill. Drawn by L. McEwan after M. Edgeworth.

that this depression had been protected after it went out of use, by the careful positioning of a large slab. Within the overlying deposits, a number of stones with incomplete perforations could have originally been the pivot stones for the driveshaft, but only one possible piece of mill stone has been recovered and analysis is awaited of this. It seems that the age-old tradition of the removal of millstones from such sites in Orkney applied even in the Norse period.

From the evidence of underlying deposits, the structure was clearly built in the Viking period, and probably had a relatively brief existence. Although it could be argued that it was not the most efficient form of milling, the type continued into the present century in the Northern Isles, of which a well-preserved example (also in stone) is the Click Mill near Dounby.[3] Fenton notes that there were 28 mills noted *c.*1600 on the Mainland of Orkney (in addition to those on the islands), including three at Orphir (one each at Kirbister, Clestrain and the Bu),[4] although it is not clear how many of these were horizontal.

In a summary of recent fieldwork, including notice of the excavation of the horizontal mill at New Mill (Fig.5), John Hunter notes that '...on Fair Isle...more tangible traditions of Norse culture manifest themselves, the yole and the mill'. In this case, it is the horizontal mill, which he states is 'introduced as a by-product of Norse culture', if not actually Norse in origin.[5] The areas of distribution of this type of mill—including Scandinavia, Orkney, Caithness/Sutherland, Outer Hebrides, Isle of Man, Shetland, Ireland, Faroe—do indeed seem to have a Norse linkage, although the Irish examples include dates prior to known Scandinavian contacts (see below), and there are also examples in the Mediterranean area (whence it is presumed the form spread). It is now quite clear from recent research by Colin Rynne on the Irish material that a non-Norse origin for the type of mill can be sustained and the term 'Norse mill' should now be rejected.[6]

The basic common features of location are, however, the strongest link: proximity to a stream in hilly or slopping terrain, connection by a millrace and sluice gate to the stream, and the head of water built up by a dam or series of dams, depending on the gradient available. Orkney's terrain is, however, markedly more gentle than that of Shetland or the Faroe Islands, and this is likely to be the main reason why horizontal mills appear to have been less common. It was usual for the best head of water to be available in the winter, when milling could take place in short bursts of time.[7] It was possibly to prevent a build-up of snow blocking the race at Orphir that the 'tunnel' was in fact covered by stone slabs.[8]

Older sources provide information on roofing materials—'thatched with peats or strips of turf'[9]—but often there are also derisive comments on the unsophisticated nature of the mechanism; Low noted that each mill was 'little better than a handmill or a quern'[10] while Hibbert castigates the grinding machinery as being 'destined for a race of pygmies'.[11] The pioneering work of Goudie on the horizontal mills of Shetland[12] remains of great significance to the study,

5. New Mill, Fair Isle. The natural stream runs at the front of the photograph, but during use was directed via a system of wooden lades across a build-up of buttressed rubble, into the mill-house. Photo J. Hunter.

providing a useful, and apparently uncoloured, commentary on the contemporary scene (Fig.6).

The dating of the Orphir mill is interesting in the Northern context. There are earlier wooden examples in Ireland,[13] but this is the first demonstrable example of the type in a Norse context of the feature sometimes termed a 'Norse mill' in the British Isles. The Irish ones include most elements of the mill structure, including wooden flumes, sluice gates and paddles or tirls, although mill races and millponds have proved elusive to locate. However, these sites have in addition the tremendous advantage of the potential for dendrochronology, as demonstrated by a recent study.[14]

This advantage is shared by the timber example which has been noted by Danish archaeologists at Omgård from the Viking period. The mill was uncovered during work on the realignment of the Pol brook in 1960, adjacent to the area of the settlement excavated in 1974–9. The sight of a water-wheel blade floating free from a disturbed area must have been amazing, and subsequent recovery of several (re-used) quernstones in that area supported initial expectations. The mill site was confirmed in 1984, and the actual position of the mill was suggested as the plateau at the junction of two head-races. Unfortunately, the mill structure seems to have been dismantled, possibly to be removed to another site. Dendrochronological dating of one phase of the mill structure suggests construction in AD 840–41.[15]

6. Surviving horizontal mill at Voe, Dunrossness, Shetland (1991). Photo C. D. Morris.

Fragments of mill stones, including imported Rhenish basaltic lava, were found on the adjacent settlement, although it is noteworthy that no such fragments were found in the mill complex. The use of garnetiferous schist querns is noted in the eleventh century at the complex.[16]

At Orphir, the added bonus has been that the stone mill structure was filled in or covered by Late Norse midden material from occupation of the nearby Bu. This has been extensively sampled throughout the work at the site, and indicates at this stage that large amounts of mammal bone with a particular emphasis on domesticates—cattle, sheep and pig, and a small amount of dog, cat and seal—can be identified.[17] Fishbone is apparently abundant, with an emphasis upon Gadids—Cod, Saithe and Pollack—and Haddock[18]. The bulk of the carbonised plant remains are vegetative, with large amounts of heather wood, leaves, shoots and flowers (some of which may indicate bedding or roofing material). Of identifiable seed material, the majority is from cereals, with some weeds. Oats are dominant, and in this aspect the assemblage is more comparable with Freswick Links, Caithness, material, than with that of Birsay Bay (where barley was dominant). Barley, when present, is probably a pure 6-row hulled variety, but there is little chaff present. Another

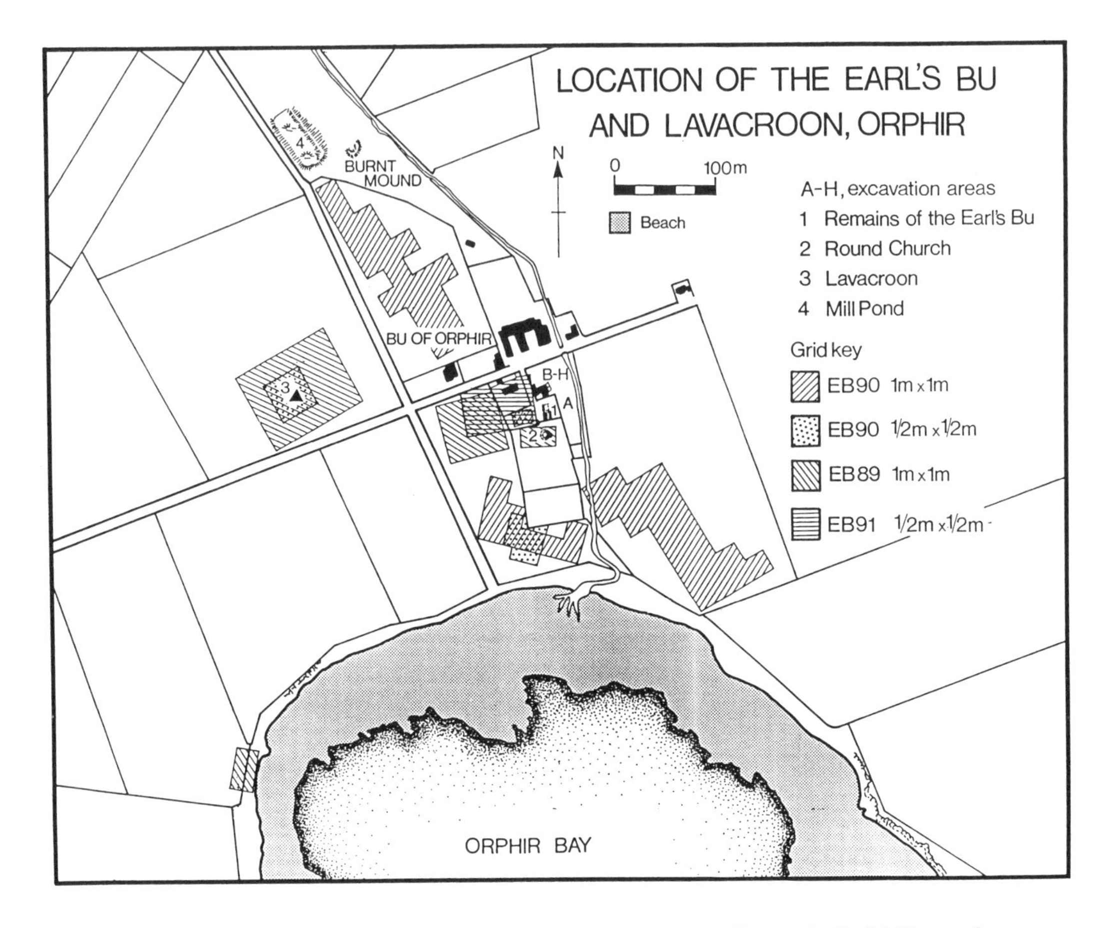

7. Location of Earl's Bu, Lavacroon and areas of geophysical survey. Drawn by L. McEwan after P. Johnson.

notable presence is that of flax which is seen in several contexts, and could possibly be locally grown; in this respect Orphir is similar to both Saevar Howe, Birsay and Pool, Sanday.[19]

Artefactual material recovered from these deposits is varied, including a steatite line sinker, whetstones, a few comb fragments and beads of Norse origin and probable Late Norse date. However, the material on which the structure is itself bedded yielded further surprises. These deposits also produced material which is Norse, potentially of earlier, Viking, date—beads, steatite vessel fragments and worked bone, as well as faunal and floral assemblages which are still to be analysed, but which will be important for comparison with the later infilling midden.

The wealth of both the artefactual and ecofactual material within the middens is exciting, and, although work is going on, there are clearly already discernible differences between the infilling material and those on which the mill is bedded. Study of all aspects will enable comparisons to be made with contemporary sites throughout the Norse Earldom of Orkney and Caithness, and into the North Atlantic sphere. The significance of all this material lies in the fact that it is the first material to be recovered from stratified contexts from the Earl's Bu site. These deposits were the debris thrown away from the 'Earl's Hall' and associated buildings; they were noted only in a cursory manner in the earlier excavations.

The complexity of the site at Orphir is not unexpected due to re-use of the stone and hence the lack of the upper part of the mill building. However, further work is needed to assist our fuller comprehension of the site as a whole: for example, the North wall of the underhouse (F14) is cut through a Bronze Age burnt mound yielding sherds of coarse food vessel, and part of the North wall of the lintelled channel is of an irregular form (F62) which might suggest alterations. Also, the relationship of the mill to the farm-mound to the South needs clarification.

The mill is a significant addition to the Earl's complex at Orphir, but this is just part of the ongoing re-appraisal of the area. Extensive geophysical work (both resistivity and magnetometry) has been undertaken by Paul Johnson on the adjacent areas (Fig.7), yielding further information about potentially Norse structures there (and possibly earlier ones too). In the area to the West of the excavation areas and the consolidated remains of the Church and Bu, there is clearly a complex palimpsest of what appear to be both buildings and curvilinear ditches. Similarly, to the South of the churchyard there are very sharp anomalies along the crest of a ridge running North-South, and traces of an earlier rectilinear enclosure(?) cut by the churchyard.[20]

Beyond this area, fieldwalking at the mound called 'Lavacroon' yielded extensive evidence of metalworking debris and Norse artefacts.[21] Subsequent geophysical work suggests the presence of very substantial structures: these would appear to be either two large circular stone constructions or one circular and one rectangular which are conjoined or partially superimposed. The area involved is in the order of 40m x 30m. It is difficult to find a Norse context for such structures.[22]

The area in the vicinity of the modern Bu Farm has been subject to severe modification over the centuries, with the addition of farm buildings and dipping tanks and also road modifications. It is difficult to imagine how the area might have looked in the Norse period. However, one feature which is clearly associated with the mill at the Bu has been examined by geophysical work, indicating features which have been partially removed during subsequent land modification. The water source for the mill may well have been brought from a pond behind a small dam to the North of the modern farm, and a strong linear anomaly has been traced which might well represent the lade. A modern mill pond, perhaps replacing an earlier one, fed the two more recent mills at the Bu Farm. The irony of this is that following a fire at the farm in 1989, the only remaining mill at the site is now the Norse one.

Acknowledgements

None of the work outlined here could have taken place without the support of Mr and Mrs J. Stephenson of Bu Farm. The assistance provided, and patience shown by them, coupled with their intuitive understanding of the importance of the site as a whole, has ensured that our time working at the site has been enjoyable as well as archaeologically stimulating.

Funding has always been a major problem for the project, particularly because of the large amount of environmental work which is an integral part of the project. However, support has been provided by the British Academy, the Societies of Antiquaries of London and Scotland, the University of Durham, the Royal Archaeological Institute, University College London, the University of Aberdeen and the Hunter Archaeological Trust. Without this support, the project could not have been undertaken to this stage, and we are most grateful to all these bodies. The work at Orphir is obviously multidisciplinary and the product of the expertise of several individuals; I must point out most specifically the work of the co-director Professor Christopher Morris and, on the environmental front, that of Mrs Jacqueline Huntley following on from James Rackham. The debt to these is immeasurable.

Notes and References

1. H. Pálsson and P. Edwards (trans), *Orkneyinga Saga*, London 1978, Ch.66, 113.
2. H. Marwick, 'Underground Galleried Building at Rennibister, Orkney', *Proc. Soc. Antiq. Scot.* LXI (1926–7), 296–301.
3. S. H. Cruden, 'The Horizontal Water-Mill at Dounby, on the Mainland of Orkney', *Proc. Soc. Antiq. Scot.* LXXXI (1947–8), 43–47.
4. A. Fenton, *The Northern Isles: Orkney and Shetland*, Edinburgh 1978, 397.
5. J. R. Hunter, 'The Multi-Period Landscape', in W. S. Hanson and E. A. Slater, eds., *Scottish Archaeology: New Perceptions*, Aberdeen 1991, 178–195.
6. A. Fenton, *op. cit.*, 396. A particularly useful discussion on various types of early mills has been published by O. Wikander, 'Archaeological, Evidence for Early Water-Mills—an Interim Report', *History of Technology, Tenth Annual Volume*, N. Smith, ed., 10 (1986), 151–179. The recent research by C. Rynne has been summarised in 'Some observations on the production of flour and meal in the early historic period', in *Journal of the Cork Historical and Archaeological Society*, XCV, No.254 (1990), 20–29.
7. Fenton, *op.cit.*
8. I am grateful for this suggestion from Peter Leith, Stenness.
9. H. Evershed, *The agriculture of the islands of Shetland*, Edinburgh 1874, 197.
10. G. Low, *A tour through the islands of Orkney and Shetland in 1774*, Kirkwall 1879, 74.
11. S. Hibbert, *A description of the Shetland Isles*, Edinburgh 1822, 19. Cited in Hunter *op.cit.*, 187.
12. Delivered to the Society of Antiquaries of Scotland in May 1886 and reprinted in G. Goudie, *The Celtic and Scandinavian Antiquities of Shetland*, Edinburgh and London 1904, 246–81.
13. See for example M. G. L. Baillie, 'A Horizontal Mill of the Eighth Century AD at Drumard, Co. Derry', *Ulster Journal of Archaeology* 38 (1975), 25–32.
14. M. [G. L.] Baillie, 'Dendrochronology—the Irish View', *Current Archaeology* 73 (1980), 61–2.; C. Rynne, 'Archaeology and the Early Irish Watermill', *Archaeology Ireland*, 3/3 (1989), 110–114.
15. L. Chr. Nielsen, 'Omgård, the Viking Age water-mill complex. A provisional report of the 1986 excavation', *Acta Archaeologica* 57 (1986), 1987, 177–210.
16. This is an interesting parallel to examples from Freswick Links, Caithness, Northern Scotland; see C. E. Batey, *Freswick Links, Caithness. A re-appraisal of the Late Norse Site in its Context*, BAR Brit. Ser. 179, 2 vols., Oxford 1987, 162–3. The probable source, in that case, is Shetland.
17. Ingrid Mainland, pers. comm.
18. James H Barrett, pers. comm.
19. Jacqueline P Huntley, pers. comm.
20. P. G. Johnson, 'The Investigation of the Environs of the Earl's Bu, Orphir, Orkney by Remote Sensing', in J. Szymanski, ed., *Proceedings of the Archaeological Sciences Conference York 1991*, forthcoming.
21. C. E. Batey with C. Freeman, 'Lavacroon, Orphir, Orkney', *Proc. Soc. Antiq. Scot.* 116 (1986), 285–300, fiche 5:A3–D9.
22. P. G. Johnson *op. cit.*

Form and Function in the Scottish Home, 1600–1950

Annette Carruthers

This paper gives a report on *Form and Function in the Scottish Home, 1600–1950*, the title of a three-year research project which started in October 1991 and is jointly organised by the National Museums of Scotland and the University of St Andrews with funding from the Leverhulme Trust.

I was appointed Leverhulme Research Fellow in July 1991. My previous experience was as a curator of decorative arts at Leicestershire and then Cheltenham Museums, where I had responsibility for period house displays and specialised particularly in nineteenth and twentieth century furniture and design, which form major elements of both museum collections. The work I have done on the Arts and Crafts Movement is quite relevant to this project. The Arts and Crafts designers were almost universally architects. They were very interested in and knowledgeable about historic building techniques and they had well-defined ideas about the home, about domestic architecture and furnishings and, to borrow the title of one of William Morris's lectures, about *How We Live and How We Might Live*.[1]

The idea for this project was conceived by John Shaw of the National Museums of Scotland and John Frew of the Art History Department at St Andrews University. They supervise the work with assistance from David Jones, also of St Andrews, and I think there are very great advantages in having a variety of approaches and skills at the supervisory level. I am based in the Science, Technology and Working Life Department at the Museum, and in the Art History Department at the University—an interesting and unusual combination!

The Museum's involvement and my own background will mean that there is much more emphasis on objects as evidence of the past than has been usual in academic research projects, and part of the aim is to provide more information about the contexts in which objects in museum collections were originally used.

The most tangible outcome will be a book. *Form and Function in the Scottish Home, 1600–1950* is the working title, which in itself suggests the method of making sense of Scottish domestic buildings and fittings by looking at the functions of the home and then seeing how these are expressed in form.

The word *home* conjures up powerful, often clichéd, images, for which the Arts and Crafts Movement is in many ways responsible. The history of the concept of home[2] is an interesting one: I hope to look at Scottish ideas about this, but I am starting with a wide view and want to look at the home in Scotland in its familiar and less usual forms—castles and country houses, tenements, classical villas, cottages, farmhouses, townhouses, lighthouses, and even less homely examples of housing. A lady from Dundee recently told me that a *howff* is a dwelling that isn't homely, like fishermen's huts and teenagers' bedrooms, and Scotland has some good examples to show in the way of lodging houses, bothies, and so on.

'Form and function' is the more complex

1. A traveller family with its *bender*, west coast of Scotland, about 1910. Photograph by M. E. M. Donaldson, Scottish Ethnological Archive, 51/18/17.

part of the title. Leaving aside for the moment the question of whether 'form ever follows function', as Louis Sullivan said[3], or whether it also defines function, the main aim is to describe the forms of the home in Scotland and to explain them in terms of the required functions of the dwelling place.

I have started by trying to define the functions. Clearly it is necessary to begin with the people, the Scots themselves and also immigrants to Scotland, from England, Ireland, Italy, Eastern Europe, Asia, and elsewhere. The functions of the home vary considerably from one person or family to the next, so that a single labourer, for instance, has very different requirements from a mother of ten. In spite of such variations, the functions of the home can be divided into groupings which seem relevant to the people and to the forms that have developed.

The first and most basic of these is shelter, epitomised by the traveller's *bender* (Fig. 1). Along with shelter I include the provision of warmth for the most basic level of survival. The wider implications in Scotland of these simple ideas include overcrowding and community spirit, and a diverse range of effects of using peat as a fuel, such as floor-level hearths and low chairs.

Next comes security. Security is not always provided by physical barriers, such as locks, doors and shutters, but also depends on factors like the constant presence of people or animals. A lack of physical forms of security can tell us much about a society and the attitudes and habits of the people.

The primary functions of the home, therefore, are to provide a sheltered and secure environment for the basics of human life: birth, procreation and death; work; and the storage, preparation and consumption of food and drink. In the past, birth and death took place in the home more frequently than they do now, while sex seems to have been more commonly an outdoor activity. Attitudes to all three have changed, and I will be looking at how these have affected the use of rooms or types of furniture. There have also been major changes in attitudes to the care of children, the sick, and the elderly, and I want to examine aspects of the institution as home for those who cannot stay in family homes.

Work in the home includes both paid work such as weaving, shoemaking, writing, painting, farming, and so on, and domestic service and unpaid household work, such as cleaning and cooking. Until this century, the home was a workplace for vast numbers of people, but the increased variety of jobs available to women gave them the chance to get out of underpaid and over-controlled work and caused the so-called 'servant problem', which formed the subject of many *Punch* cartoons in the 1920s and '30s.

This had a major effect on the form of household furnishings, the development of household equipment, and the use of rooms—for instance, transforming middle-class kitchens from the bleak area fit only for servants to the cosy, country-style, family kitchen beloved of *Ideal Home*.

Until the beginning of the nineteenth century, a wider range of people worked at home or in workshops attached to the home, and their removal to factories and business offices changed attitudes to what the home was for. To the middle-class man it became a haven from the dirty world of commerce, and the

2. Interior at Larchgrove House, Balerno, about 1897. Scottish Ethnological Archive, C11197.

'sweet sanctities of domestic life'[4] came to be seen as the woman's sphere. She was the angel of the hearth, whether she liked it or not (Fig. 2).

Along with work in the home, I include work on the home; it is surprising how much energy was expended in re-making roofs and walls and cutting peat for fuel for rural houses in Scotland.

The provision of food can have an enormous effect on the form of houses and household goods, and the number and range of rooms depend on the types and quantities of food stored and used. Factors such as the availability of shops or the proximity of vegetable gardens will influence the form of the dwelling, and the provision of food as entertainment leads on to the next function of the home: as a place for recreation and leisure and celebration of the occasions of life.

In two-room dwellings all over Scotland there was usually a Best Room for entertaining visitors (where visitors were very rarely invited in), and in larger houses there were dining rooms, billiard rooms, smoking rooms, and so on, all with their own distinctive features. Then there were buildings devoted solely to leisure pursuits: weekend cottages, hunting lodges, holiday caravans and suchlike, and forms of temporary housing for business or pleasure, like hotels. All had forms of their own and their very existence also affected the nature of more permanent dwellings in a variety of ways.

These functions are fairly straightforward. Rather more nebulous, but undeniably important, is the idea of the house as evidence of status—of the occupant's position in society. Sometimes this is made plain through the grandeur of the architecture, and sometimes it shows in more subtle ways, like the shiny brass letterbox which proclaims cleanliness, godliness, and respectability, or the display of prized possessions. Inside the house, the arrangement and furnishing of rooms reflects status considerations in ways which are so familiar we take them for granted—the best carpet in the living room, plainer mouldings and skirtings in the bedrooms—and even when unfurnished, it is usually possible to tell what a room is for from its decoration. But these things change, and for an understanding of the past we have to learn the rules: dining-room fireplaces, for instance, were usually black in nineteenth-century Edinburgh townhouses, while drawing-room fireplaces were generally light coloured, of finer statuary marble.

The notion of form defining function occurs interestingly in relation to status. Buildings can have an overawing effect on people and this influences their behaviour. Architects can contrive such effects, and home owners can use architects as a means of acquiring status.

My last category of function is probably the most difficult to define and to contain: it is the idea of the home as an expression of spiritual values. The creation of a chapel as part of the house is an obvious example, but the creation of a beautiful room as a means of expressing personal creativity is another. This can bring in the role of interior decorators and furnishers, and also the meanings implicit in certain colour combinations or decorative motifs: a cream-coloured room with flowered curtains, for instance, speaks of different values from a grey one with Venetian blinds.

The creation of a home is often bound up with complex feelings about family life, and with wider affiliations, regional and national. It may not be possible to explain entirely, but why are there, for instance, distinct differences between Edinburgh and Glasgow tenements? Are some features there to demonstrate local affinities, as some homes clearly show a sense of Scottishness?

Osbert Lancaster's view of Scottish Baronial in *Homes Sweet Homes*[5] demonstrates how easy it is to make a joke of this, but the conscious adoption of a Scottish identity by the Scots raises questions about the development of an understanding of Scotland's history, of antiquarianism and antique collecting—and inevitably such figures as Sir Walter Scott, whose passion for collecting from the past was combined with an enthusiasm for the most modern technology, like gas lighting and pneumatic bell-pushes.

Scott's house, Abbotsford, is also interesting in the context of spiritual aspects of the home, as an example of a house preserved as a shrine to a great Scottish figure.

Beyond Scottishness, I am hoping to find some evidence of the influence on the home in Scotland from Scots who have been abroad and returned, or from immigrants from other countries.

Clearly, the subject of the Scottish home is too big for one person to cover in three years, so I am attempting to gather together research that others have been working on over some time. The book will consist of introductory chapters on function and other factors which influence form, and a series of articles by other people covering a range of building types—such as cottages, tenements, townhouses, institutions, and so on. Because most scholars study either an architect and contemporaries, or a fairly short timespan, and because a chronological approach suits the arrangement of photographs in a book, this main section will be roughly in date order, starting at 1600.

I have been very impressed by the wide-ranging research going on in Scotland among architectural historians, furniture historians, museum curators, and others. There has been a series of day meetings of lectures by such people, which I hope will contribute to thinking about the subject. The first, in November 1992, was on the conditions in Scotland which affect the development

3. Interior at 84 Causeyside Street, Paisley, about 1900. From an unusual collection of photographs of working-class interiors at Paisley Museum and Art Galleries, Renfrew District Council, 78/11.

of the home: the landscape and climate, the availability of building materials, the development of building technology and services, the provisions of Scots Law and so on. The second, in December, was on sources of evidence and how to interpret them, such as paintings, literature, oral history, film, and archives. Subsequent meetings dealt with Scottish material culture and the furniture and furnishings of the home.

My own part of the research will be on urban and industrial working-class housing in Lowland Scotland of about 1830–1919 (Fig. 3) and about ideas for improvement, such as reformed tenements, colonies, and the cottage-style housing and garden suburb arrangements which were usually developed by Arts and Crafts architects from the English vernacular and infiltrated into Scotland from the south.

In order to make the whole project more permanently useful to others, I am collecting information on relevant museum, library, and archive collections and sites, and I hope to record this on a database. I am also interested in any images of Scottish homes that are not already well-known and am acquiring photographs to add to the Scottish Ethnological Archive at the National Museums of Scotland. Any information will be very welcome.

References

1. Lecture delivered in 1884, A. L. Morton, ed., *Political Writings of William Morris* (London 1979), 134–58.
2. See, for instance, J. Calder, *The Victorian Home* (London 1977) and W. Rybczynski, *Home: A Short History of an Idea* (London 1988).
3. L. H. Sullivan, 'The Tall Office Building Artistically Considered', *Lippincott's Magazine*, March 1896.
4. J. W. Burgon, *To Educate Young Women Like Young Men,—A Thing Inexpedient and Immodest, A Sermon* (Oxford 1884), 17 (quoted in J. N. Burstyn, *Victorian Education and the Ideal of Womanhood* (New Brunswick 1984), 32).
5. O. Lancaster, *Homes Sweet Homes* (London 1939), 40–1.

The Diary of a Gardener at Skaill, Orkney: 3 January–7 May 1801

Nancy Hewison

Gardening in Orkney has always posed particular problems. The scattered islands are comparatively low-lying and thus exposed to winds from every quarter. The sea is nowhere more than four miles distant and the most fertile land is often on the coast itself so that salt-burn is added to the ferocity of the frequent gales. This is especially damaging as growth is often early owing to the relatively frost-free maritime climate.

Shelter of some sort is a necessity—provided in planticrues (walled enclosures) by the small farmers—but by the seventeenth century the larger estates had walled gardens similar to those further south in Scotland and England. A plan of the Earls' Palace at Birsay, undated but probably early seventeenth century, shows the lay-out of the grounds—'the Floure yard, the Herb yard, the Keall yard and the Planti Yard'—all enclosed and sheltered from the sea by the bulk of the palace itself; but that garden is no longer in existence.

The garden at Skaill House, about seven miles to the south, does exist though neglected and overgrown, and may be only slightly later in date. The oldest part of the house was built by Bishop George Graham of Breckness at the beginning of the seventeenth century. A stone unearthed in the garden bore the date 1633. The garden may well have been contemporary. It was certainly an old garden when William Watt, a prosperous Kirkwall merchant, acquired the property in 1787 from the brother of his second wife, Margaret Graham, daughter of Robert Graham of Breckness.

Lying midway along the rock-bound west coast of the Orkney Mainland where the cliffs are broken by a broad sandy bay—the *Sand-Vik* of the Norsemen - Skaill House takes its name from the Old Norse *skáli*, a hall, which previously occupied the site on the links between the bay and the freshwater loch all of which now share the same name, Skaill. The Stone-age village of Skara Brae which lies a few hundred yards away testifies to the area's popularity as a place of settlement for a few millennia before the Norsemen.

The soil is very light and sandy and must have benefited greatly from the copious applications of animal manure mentioned in this manuscript Diary of the gardener, Hugh Ross.

The Diary is now in the Scottish Record office, Edinburgh, ref: GD 31/445. Ross's letter of application for the post of gardener at Skaill is among the Skaill Collection of papers held in the Orkney Archives in Kirkwall (ref: OA D3/37). It reads as follows:

> Hugh Ross to Mr William Watt Esq, Breakness.
>
> Hounered Sir,
>
> I take upon me to write your houner these few lines,—hounered sir. I am a native of Loch Aber and a gardner bred and I served Colonel McDonald of Boisdle south Uist for 12 months as gardner and left him last

> Martimas and now I took my passage along with a vesel bound to Leith & and (sic) came this lenth a board of her and monday night as I was a shore he went off in the neight time and carried all my cloths along with him and left myself also and now as I heard your houner had no gardner I thought proper to offer myself to you
>
> I am Sir yours Hugh Ross.

The garden seems to have fallen into neglect by the time he started work in January 1801—as it has done again today. It measures 120 feet square enclosed by massive walls of local stone—that on the north side being 10 foot high with a 7 foot high wall on the east and south sides but only 5 foot on the west, but this side is sheltered by the rambling mansion house which has been added to several times over the years even in the present century. The paths and borders, edged with flag stones, are clearly visible today even under the growth of thistles, docks and nettles. The paths are 4 feet in width and the borders vary from 9 to 5 feet, and in the centre it is possible to detect the outline of some beds.

Hugh Ross's labours ended with his death only four months after he was first employed, but whether he died suddenly after an accident or after an illness it has been impossible to establish so far. The burial records for the parishes of Sandwick and Stromness for that year are missing, and a search of the business and personal papers of William Watt have yielded no information about his servant's death.

There is a curious change in the handwriting and style of the diary towards the end, perhaps through illness. As well as Ross's individualistic spelling, he is somewhat careless with dates. February is given 29 days although 1801 is not a leap year, but as though to compensate, March has only 30 days.

Among interesting points is the reference on 29 April to '. . . transplanting melons from *the gavel of the house* to the hot bed'. This was a bed of earth heated by fermenting manure, which may also have been covered with glass, a practice known in England at least from the early eighteenth century.

The Orkney lairds, including the Watts, seem to have been busy planting trees at this period but none of the fir or larch mentioned seems to have succeeded. Skaill and its surroundings are certainly bare of trees today although these and other species have succeeded elsewhere in Orkney.

The number of different vegetables is surprising, and some plants such as *elecampane* may have had medicinal uses. *Cammicel* is puzzling: the second -c- could be read as -e-, and the word may therefore be camomile.

The firm of Wm Watt, Jnr & Company certainly imported a great many seeds from, amongst others, Dickson & Co, Seedsmen, Edinburgh, and the Orkney Archive also holds some orders placed and supplied by the Watts to many other Orkney landowners at a slightly earlier date. One example dated 13 April 1774 is more a cry from the heart: '. . . if you have time send the flower seeds—a kind of large mice as big as rats have destroyed all my fine flowers of which I was so proud'.

The writer of these introductory notes has also suffered from the attentions of the Orkney mole!

The full text of the Journal is as follows:

'Journal of Work done in the Garden of Skaill by Hugh Ross as Gardner'.[1]

1801, Jan 3rd – I Hugh Ross this day entered the service of Mr William Watt Esq of Breckness to work in his Garden as Gardner

9th – I this day have begun my proposels, with an half hours assistance of George More wrought on whilling [wheeling] the earth out of the west Walk all this day

10th – Before breckfast Thomas Hervy drove two Cart's of horse dung to the south door and I wrought at whilling the west Walk all the day

11th – Sunday was a very pleasent dry day with a south wind

12th – I wrought till Eleven O'Clock and no longer it being the first day of the new year

13th – I was sick all this day did nothing

14th – I wrought till ten O'Clock and

then went to Stromness where I continued till night

15th – I wrought all this day at whilling the west Walk till night

16th – I wrought on whilling the earth out of the west walk all the day

Jan 17th – till twelve O'Clock I wrought on whilling the earth out of the west walk and than till night dressing the Archcockes.

18th – Sunday which was a very pleasent dry day till after sermon, and then it began snowy shours and continued till Night

19th – Till ten O'Clock I was dressing the Archicocke and then went to the Munt (the name for the farm buildings of Skaill) and drove 2 Carts of horse dung and then whelled that in on the Archicockes and at three O'Clock went to Strumness

20th – Till ten O'Clock I wrought on deging the Archicockes and then after Breckfast I was whilling dung on them till about one O'Clock and then went up to the Munt and Ordered John Corrigall to drive a Cart of Clay, after that I was keep'd within with a sever South west shoor of sleet which continued blowing very hard all the night Over.

21st – The storm yesterday still continued all this Day, I did no thing but nail'd two Apples trees in the midle of the day

22nd – I was dressing the wall trees till Breckfast and then I took up the Bullbous rooted plant as much as I could find of them and took them in, and then I went and dugg what was undug of the Archicocks Thomas Hervy & John Corrigall drove a Cart of horse dung each of them

23rd – This morning they Came a great draft of snow and has continued all this day and stoped from doing any thing but only that I took in a small store of Cabbage and Carrot

24th – I went to the Miln in the morning and was helping to set it agoing as it stoped after last nights frost and then went to Stromness along with Mr Robert and turned over all the hyds that was in the ware house

25th – Being Sunday, I took in a small parsel of parsneps and in the midle of the day it came on a south wind and took on a very good frish thaugh which carried off all the snow it shoored the two last past Days

26th – George More drove four Cart loads of Clay in the midle of the day and I was nailing the trees all the day could do very little with a very cold North West (frosty) wind

27th – The day being a deal more suverer than yeasterday I did very little but asusted in yoking the two sholties in the Cart and John Taylor drove three Carts of horse dung with the[m] my whill barrough brock then wh[ich] stoped me from doing any more this night

28th – The frost being hard and more snow fell last night I did nothing till Ten O'Clock and then I nailed two small trees and after that I went and got John Taylor and yoked the two sholties, and he and I, we drove six Cart loads of horse dung

29th – It came a great thaugh last night from the east and continued all this day which stoped me doing any thing this day but only I took up a few Carrot to denner

30th – The Frost came on again and has continued all this day and I did nothing worth mentioning but took in some carrots and Cabbage

31st – The morning being still frosty I did nothing till ten O'Clock, and then I went to the Milner with the while of the whilebarro till get it mended and afwards [sic] went to the smith with three peices of an old Cart bolt and got it bet out and made a new gurd for the wheel

Feb. 1st – Being Sunday a very great thaw came last night which put the Miln in danger and I wrought some on defending the watter which decressed about two O'Clock

2nd – I went this morning and got the whiel ended which keep'd till twelve O'Clock and then John Taylor yoked the Cart and drove Eleven Carts of stones and I wheeled them in on the walk

3rd – In the morning I wheel'd in the remainder of the stones Carted yesteday till ten O'Clock and then James Hervie yoked the Cart and drove Eleven Cartloads as yesterday and I followed in wheeling all the day

4th – Till ten O'Clock I wheel'd in stones and than I went along with John Taylor and took two load of earth from the smith's Garding and a load of Clay for the Hot beds and then wheel'd in stones till night. John

Taylor Drove six Carts of stone and Thomas Hervey drove five load of horse dung

5th – Till ten O'Clock I was wheeling in stones and gathered the Potato Crops and burnt them and then Prooned some Apple and Goosberrie plants in the north border till Night

6th – I was prooning The Goosberrie plants till two O'Clock then I went and planted seven balsome Poplars and four wollos [willows] in the little park and then I was whelling in stones till Night. John Taylor drove two load of horse dung to the south door and eight load of stones with the sholties

7th – Till ten o'clock I was wheeling in stones and then till Denner time I was wheeling in sand and then assisted in puting up the flages to the north wall. John Taylor drove 1 load of horse dung, 2 of stone and 9 of sand

8th – Sunday which was a very musty *day* [scored out] all the whole day with rain

9th – In the morning I was planting & prooning Goosberrie pushes and after Breckvast I was assisting in puting up flags to the North wall with Mr William Mr Robert & the Milner. John Taylor drove one cart of horse dung, two of clay & six of stones, and Thomas Scolai was wheeling out rubbage off the walks George More was lousing the stones of the North Walk after denner John Charles asisted a little in the Eving about one flag & fulled up some holes in the wall

10th – Till Breckvast I was p[r]ooning & gathering cuttings of Bor-tree and then sucked (soaked) them, and after that I went with Thomas Scolai to take up some carrot where he remained all the Day and I went and wheel'd six barroug full of Clay & four of dung on the North border & then dug it, George More was lousing the stones and wheeled some of them to the Gravel walk. John Taylor drove eight load of Clay from the rocks

11th – I[n] the morning I was planting the Bulbous rooted plants into North Border and planted a sma[?] Edgen of None-so-prety than I wheeled in some Barroughs of Clay & Dung and then dug it and then sowed Cabbage, Hasties[?] (early peas) & Radishes in the North B. John Taylor drove Eight load of stones. Thomas Scollie ended the lifting the carrot this day

12th –This day was a fast day and I did nothing, but went to Stromness on my own bussiness along with Mr Robt

13th – In the Morning I was wheeling in Clay & dung to the North Border, & after Breckfast I dug what I dung'd in the morning then I was Planting Bulbous perenial and Herbaches Plants in the place I dug after denner (with the assistance of the men) I was putting up flags till night. John Taylor drove five load of horse dung and five of stones

14th – I sunk ten flags and dressed the pits of them to the north wall to plant the fruite trees in the rest of day I was With the assistance of the men setting up flags to the north wall till night

Feb 15th – Sunday was a very warm day in the morning I took off the mats of the seeds and at night laid them on

16th – till ten O'Clock I was wheeling in stones on the walk and then I was wheeling in dung and C[l]ay on the north Border and was digging on it till night

17th – Till ten O'Clock I was dunging & claying the north Border then dug it then with the assistance of Mr William I was setting up flags, then I planted out Carrots for seed, then I was planting Bulbous, Perenial & Harbaches plants, John Taylor drove four load of horse dung to the South door

18th – Till ten O'Clock I was planting Goosberries and Currents in the border aside the Gravel walk, then I rooted out two rows of Cabbage and drew a path then I got twenty of the best Cabbage stoks and shoched them for seed then I gathered some cuttings of bore tree and shoched them I then planted bolbous Perenial & Herbaetious plants which finished the north border I then was wheeling in stones till night

19th – I was all this day wheeling in stones to the Gravel walk and woud have finished it if I had stones enough

20th – Till ten O'Clock I was wheeling in Clay on the Border that I planted the 18th Int then John Taylor drove one Cart of stones I wheel'd it in and took the rest from the north border and finished that part of the walk then went to the shore along with the boys and took up Gravel till night

21st – In the morning I was spreding the *dung* [scored out] Clay I wheeled yeasterday then John Taylor was d[r]iving the sand to the Cravel [sic] walk and I was fulling the Cart along with him we drove one Cart of Gravel from the shore & eight of sand the [sic] turned out very blowey and and [sic] rain and stoped me from doing any thing more this day

22nd – Sunday this day was a good day, fair day with south east wind

23rd – Till midday I was wheeling in sand on the Gravel walk then I was whee[l]ing in Chingle till tow O'Clock then nailed a Cherrie Tree to the west wall then I was preparing to riddle the Earth for the hot Beds John Taylor drove one lod of horse dung & six of Chingle from the shore

24th – First I riddled some earth for the hot Beds then I was Cutting the edge of the walk dunging & diging the south border all the day John Taylor drove five load of Clay and nine of dung from Hugh Bues byer

25th – *All this day was* [scored out] The wind S.E. with rain continued all day. I did very little only I wheeled in ten barroughful of dung to the Eeast border and dug a very little

26th – The wind NW with very severe Shours of rain & Continued all day. I sunk nine flags in the West border and dug a very little on the East Do

27th – In the morning I was planting Turnep & Cabbage stocks for seed in the east border then I dug and dunged it the remainder of it Then I was wheel[ing] dung on the west border and dug on it till there cam a sudent shou[r] of rain and Stoped all this night

28th – All this Day I was dunging & deging the west border. John Taylor drove one load of horse dung and six of Cow Do Chay mo pheysger car Chag in due.[2]

29th – Sunday this day was a very bad day S W Rain all the day I was in Strumness & receved a Letter from Mess. Dicksons & Co & one from my father

March 1st – In the morning I dressed the ground to the east side of the gravel walk for the edgen then planted it then planted the border with herbachous, perenial, & beinial plants. James hervey drove 4 load of C[l]ay John Corigall one load of Cow dung John Talyor drove 1 of Cow & 2 of horse Do. I was at the loch asisting in launching the plasure boat this being the first time she was afloat this season

2nd – Till ten O'Clock I was dressing Cutings of sorts that came from Kirkwall then was rooting out old Cabbage stocks, wheeled them out and cleared one for the part of the 1st plote for the cutings then was wheeling in dung on it, then got a roul[?] made

3rd – the plasure boat went off to nigh[t] the first thing I did this morning was to go and secure her then was wheeling in dung and deging all this day on the plote I cleared yeaster Day

4th – Till ten O'Clock I was degen the same plot as yesterday then I was planting willows & bore tree cutings in the south border

March 5th – Till ten O'Clock I was planting willows & Bortree cuting then dunging & deging on the 1st plot till night

6th – Till two O'Clock I was deging on the 1st plot then planted *100* [scored out] hundred of Cabbage then planted 600 Goosberries & Currant cutings in the 1st plot

7th – Sunday wind S W with a soor [sic] of rain all the day

8th – till ten O'Clock I did nothing as the morning was snowing very hard from the north after ten I was deging & dressing the side of the set

9th – In the morning I was wheeling in dung on the west border after that I was planting cabbage till night John Taylor drove 20 load of cow dung betwen satterday and the day

March 10th – Till ten O'Clock I was planting Cabbage then I was deging the west wall Border & dunging it till night.

11 th – Till two O'Clock I was deging the border as yeasterday and finished it the[n] I drew a path across the plot from the north wall to the mid walk

12th – Till two O'Clock I was planting perenial & herbachious plants then it began with shours of rain which stoped me from doing anything more this night

13th – they came a fall of snow last night I could do nothing in the Garding but went to Mr Clouston's with some straberries plants and planted them there and got home with me some deices and other flower plants

14th – Sunday the snow still continues but is a very pleasent day

15th – this day the snow is as yeasterday but there is a thaw with shours of rain which stoped me from doing any thing of consequence but wheeled in some barroughs of chingle on walk

16th – till two O'Clock I was planting a edgen of deices to the west side of the gravel walk then I was planting Current bushes on the south side of Garden till night

17th – till two O'Clock I was trenching the walk then the night came out so bade I could not work out but cut a anker of Potatoes for seed

18th – the morning being bade I did nothing till ten O'Clock then I was trenching as yeasterday till two then was tosting up dung for our hot beds till night

19th – till 2 O'Clock I was transplanting Cabbage for greens & there was four woman bearing dung to the plot Where we are to plant our Potatoes then the night came out with very suver wind and rain when we were all oblidge to abandon our work

20th – till ten O'Clock I was rooting up Cabbage stocks then planted some for greens then was wheeling out stoks and tosting up the dung till two then we were called in to denner and went with buirrial which ended this night

21st – Sunday was a very rainy day from the North

22nd – till ten O'Clock I did nothing the morning being very snowy till denner time I was rooting up Cabbage roots and wheeling them out, till night I was trenching more till night on the east walk

23rd – till ten O'Clock I did nothing the morning being very frosty then there came three bearrers and I was fulling on them for about three hours then I was deging the right hand border from the doer [door] till night

24th – this morning being very rainy I did nothing till ten O'.C. then I was deging the border aside the Archicocks till denner time then I was Obledge to give it up for the rain

25th – till *the* [scored out] ten O'Clock I was wheeling in dung on the north border then I planted the Cammicel [Camomile?] in the right hand border then I deded [sic] the left hand border then I began to deg the border that goes north and continued till night

26th – till twelve O'clock I was deging and dressing the edge of the border then was deging the ground for the Potatoes with assistance of John Charles from denner time till night

27th – till 10 O'Clock with the asistance of John Charles we were digging the Potatoe ground till 2 O'Clock Thos Scollay and my self was planting them then trenching till Night—amen

28th – Sunday being a very good Day we had no sermen

29th – All this Day I was planting and Degging the north strabberry border

30th – till 10 O'Clock I was degging the south border and planting Cabbage in it then with the asistance of Joh[n] Charles I made the Nurcirie hot bed

1st Aprile – first I earth'd the Nurcerie bed then planted a row of flowers in the left hand border then planted 3 Hundred Cabbage in rows in the borders then was spreding the dung that 4 bearrers beared in this day then tosted up the remainer of the dung telt[?] by the Nurcerie hot bed

2nd – till ten O'Clock I was Celleary, Cabbage, Coliflower, & Turnip in the north border There was two men and John Charles degging all this Day I went to Stromness along with 4 men for 27 flower pots and planted 7 Apple trees for John Louttit[3]

3rd – till ten O'Clock I was dressing the ground that was dug yeasterday then Thomas Scollie planted the early potatoes and some of the red topit[?] kind I was sowing Onion, Carrot, Parsnep & Cabbage seed, the day being very misty all day then cam on rain I did nothing more this day

4th – I went very early to Stromness and sowed Onions, Carrots, parsneps, Radish, Lattice, Liek, Pease, Parsilie, Cresse & Kidney Beens to John Louttet being a very bad snowy day when I came home Sowed the Coucumber & mellon seed in the Nurcirie bed

5th – sunday being as suvere a day with frost and snow as came this twomonth past

6th – till 1 O'Clock I was in the smidy getting a rack (rake) made I then trenched 4 trenches of the walk then went and gave a rough raking to the seed bede I sowed by day which ended this day being a very course day also

7th – this day being very suvere and snowy I did very little but took care of the hot bed gathered one hundred straberries plants to Mr Robert and planted 7 plants in pots

8th – Till Dinner time I was dressing earth for the hot Bed, then sowed some white and Brown Mustard and some Kidney Beans and Pease. Being a verry bad day

Apr 9th – Till Brakefast time I was at the Smiddy getting the garden Reel repaired, after Brakfast was puting Earth upon the South Border then Planting out Rhubarb and Elicampane. There were four women dunging the N E plot

10th – With the asisstance of two men William Inkestr & George Groundwater we were deging on the N E plot all day, the day being very course with shours of sleat from N W

11th – Could do but verry little but Trenching the Day being verry bad, with Shours of sleet from the N W

12th – Sunday weather as usual til Twelve O'Clock When the wind turned to N E

13th – Til dinner time Lining out the N E Plot for the Cabbage then planted 400 plants in it wind W. continual Rain all day

14th – All this day with the Assistance of Thomas Scollie was planting the N E plot with Cabbage, wind W thick must with shours of rain all day

15th – till 2 O'Clock was leaveling the east walk then dug the border for Mrs Bain's Potatoes. wind W thick must but very warom all day

16th – dug the ground for the following Potatoes No 2 cut the common way No 3 the whole Way No 4 cut the long way No 5 cut in two halfs then smoth raked the first crop of Onions, Carrots & Parsnep then dressed some of the Straberries & shooch'd the natherin [?] wind W. till twelve O'clock and thick must then changed east which cleard the must away being very warom all day

17th – till 2 O'Clock was dressing the straberries then was chaghing Cabbage till night, wind E & S by S till about 12 O'Clock then S.W being a very warom day

18th – Went to Stromness and raked the seeds I sowed to John Louttet & sow'd more Onions, Leik & Beens Wind S till 2 O'Clock—W & by S with a fall of rain all the evening

19th – Sunday rain till ten O'Clock & Wind S W then wind W cleared up and continued fair all night

20th – till ten O'Clock was wheeling in clay on the Onion ground, was then dressing the borders, there was 13 bearrers the day some shours of rain wind, W

21st – till 2 O'Clock was degging the Onion ground then was sowing Onions, radishes & Lattices John Charles was wheeling in some barows of clay and dung Wind W & by N a very warom day

22nd – With the assistance of Will Inkstire was deging the seed ground and sowed three beds of Onions Kitty Spence was bearring dung for us. Wind very changeable from E to South

23rd – Was sowing Parsnips Carrots Radishes Cellerrie & Couliflower then dugg a little Wind W & by S

24th – Was degging till 2 O'Clock then sowed some Carrot Wind S.E.

25th – Went off this morning along with James Rogland to the moss hill and marked out the moss then came home about 2 O'Clock then after denner I sow'd Yellow Turnip & turnep Radish Wind S. E.

26th – sunday a very hot day Wind S. W.

27th – till 2 O'Clock was raking the Onions then sow'd 6 dreels of Turnep & 2 beds of pease the [sic] was very hot Wind till 2. E & by S then—W

28th – till ten O'clock was atending the hot bed then went to the Mount & was trenching the earth for the fire & Larch tree seed a strong gall of wind S & by E

29th – till ten O'clock was transplanting the Melons from the geval of the house to the hot bed then was raking the remainder of the Onions then went to the Mount and harrowed the ground for the fir seeds, a strong gell of wind S. E.

30th – till 10 O'Clock was howing the south plote of Cabbage then went to the Mount and dung'd & dug the ground for the fir, a strong wind as Yeasterday S. E.

May 1st – till ten O'clock was sowing the Fir and Larch seed then till night was building the Fence across the barnyard, a strong gall of wind S.

2nd – till two O'Clock was building the fence at the mount then was howing till Night wind S. E.

3rd – Sunday Calm and very hot

4th – till two O'Clock was sowing & dressing the east walk then was houghing till Night Calm & hot

5th – till 10 O'clock was houghing then till denner was raking and dressing the borders then went to the sheep's fould and was shoveling the sand from the daek then was taking up the lint [?] mati[..]ry from the shore till the barn a very sharp brice of wind E & by S with a shour of rain in the morning

6th – was all this day in Seetter planting boretree & hawthorn wind with shours of rain a[s] yeasterday all the day

7th – was all this day building the fence wind as yeasterday very cold but no shours planted 2 Mellons & 2 Couckemers in a bot [pot] for Mr Robert to send to Kirk-wall.

Notes

1. Subscription on cover: *Journal of Work done in the Garden of Skaill by Hugh Ross as Gardner commencing 3rd Jany 1801 and ending 7th May 1801 by his death. Lodged in the Clerks hand for Benefit of all concerned, General Register House, Edinburgh, Reference GD 31/445.*
2. Gaelic: 'Chaidh mo fheasgar car cac an-diugh', my afternoon/evening went/turned rather shitty today. Thanks are due to Donald Archie MacDonald, School of Scottish Studies, for advice.
3. There was no road between Stromness and Skaill at this period. Journeys would have had to be made on horseback, but goods would have come by boat. This is confirmed by a letter in the Orkney Archives, ref. D3/27, from John Louttit, Stromness to Wm. Watt, Skaill, dated 2 April 1801, dealing with business matters and '. . . The flower pots is Sent by your Boat and also the Directions I got with them . . . I have used the freedom to keep your Gardner all Night to Set a few Trees I have got down from England, and also to sow some Seeds As Hugh Ross says he cannot stay down with us all night on acct of Some Seeds he has to sow in a Hoat Bed this evening. I will esteem it as a favour if you will be so good as to let him come down on Saturday morning to Sow Some Seeds for us as we can get none here that can do it and Send me by him the Carrot Seeds I formerly wrote you for and if possible Spare me one peck of Rye Grass and a Pound of White Clover.'

Footnote. The frequently mentioned 'Mr William' and 'Mr Robert' were the sons of William Watt by his first wife. 'Mrs Bain' was his daughter by the first wife. Most of the other names are common in the parish today.

Reparations to the Workflows: Eighteenth-Century Garden Tools

A. D. Boney

Summary

'Worklooms' to the Scots gardener of olden times were the tools of his trade. Whilst the costings of new implements are often to be found in the accounts of sizeable gardens,[1] the running repairs ('reparations') are less obvious. As always, gardeners were expected to 'make do' with well-used tools for as long as possible. Repair bills from the past give insights both into the reliability of the various implements, and sometimes into attendant working conditions. Some such insights are available for the seventeenth and eighteenth century gardens of the University of Glasgow.

Introduction

The gardens formed part of the 'Old College' on its medieval site south of the Cathedral (Fig. 1). The walled Great Garden was some nine Imperial acres in area. It was quartered and bounded by grassed walks (Fig. 2). The walks were carpeted with a mixture of rye grass and dwarf white clover, and lined with trees and flowering shrubs. The four 'plots' were studded with a variety of fruit trees, and these were also planted against the walls. These 'plots' were covered with rye grass mixed with red clover. There was a small Physic Garden, less than three-quarters of an Imperial acre in area, and essentially a teaching adjunct. It contained a number of plants of medicinal value, along with some decorative ones. A number of vegetables were also grown—possibly a professorial 'perk'. The Great Garden was for the exclusive recreational use of the professors. The only students permitted to share the amenities were those 'of noble birth'. The general student body were not admitted until the late 1770s—and then were only allowed to walk about. Running, jumping, or playing ball games resulted in fines and banishment from using the gardens. The Great Garden was leased to local townsmen (not necessarily gardeners), who made what profits they could from the sale of grass cuttings and fruit in the town. In this way the professors ensured the regular cutting of the walks and the plots throughout the growing seasons, and the proper annual care of the fruit trees. All such requirements were carefully written into the contracts for the tacks (leases). In the latter half of the eighteenth century the professors became more involved in the management of the Great Garden, especially the plantings.

A succession of gardeners were appointed, primarily with responsibility for running the small Physic Garden, but in time having some overseeing responsibilities for the Great Garden as well. The repairs to their implements are included in the annual accounts submitted by a number of tradesmen employed by the University—the hammermen (smiths), wrights (carpenters), and sometimes the masons. The charges for such repairs lie hidden in their accounts amongst a wide variety of other jobs carried out. It was a rare event for such a garden repair job to be a single item. Overall, 140 tradesmen's accounts and receipted bills or precepts,

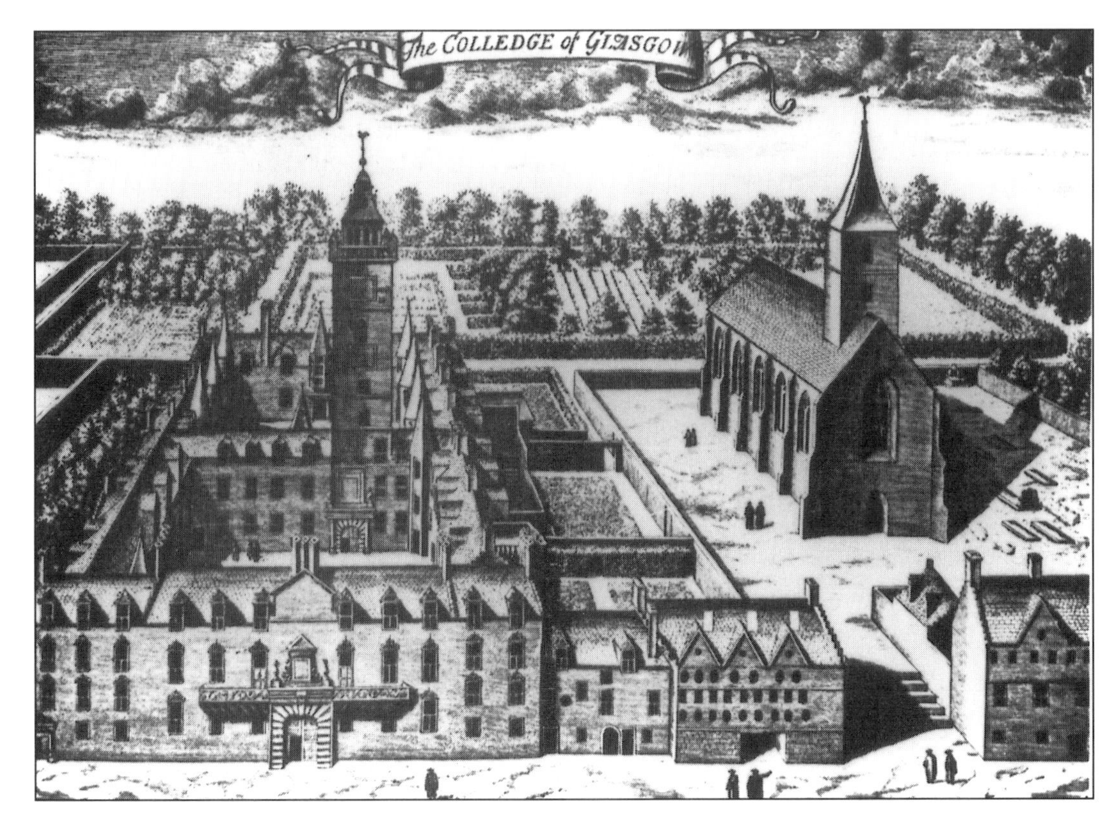

1. Slezer's engraving of the 'Old College' of the University of Glasgow on its medieval site, with the Great Garden to the rear. The engraving was published in 1693 but the original drawing was of an earlier date. The Physic Garden did not exist at that time.

starting from 1656, have been examined. In the following all the costings are given in sterling. In the original accounts they were in Scots money, in sterling, and sometimes a mixture of both (£1 Scots = one twelfth of £1 sterling). The variable spelling in the old Scots will be included on occasions, with interpretations where necessary.

Rolling Stones

The rolling stones were amongst the most frequently quoted items for repairs. In October 1656 the University paid a local quarrier 3/4d for 'hewing twa rolling stanes for ye Gardene'.[2] James Johnstone, a hammerman, presenting his annual bill to the University in April 1656, included two items for rollers. He charged 2/0d for fitting 'twa grate iron batts', and 11/8d for 'Ye iron work at dressing ye roller'. 'Batts' were iron bars or battens forming parts of the frame, and 'dressing' referred to general, and in this case quite extensive, repair work.[3] The frames of the rollers occupied the attentions of a succession of hammermen over the years. John Black regularly included some repair detail in his annual accounts from 1723 to 1737. On 17 April 1723 he charged 3/0d for 'twa gwgans (gudgeons) and twa eies (eyes) for the timber rower for 'the rowing of ye walks of ye big yeard (Great Garden)'. Two days later a similar repair for 'a lesser rower' cost 1/10d.[4] Charges were based on weights of metal used. In the first repair 8lb 8oz of iron were used, and 5lb 8oz for the second, equal to about one farthing per ounce of metal, including labour costs. The gudgeons were metal pivots fitted into the solid ends of the rollers, and the eyes were metal rings fitted into cavities in the roller ends through which the gudgeons passed. Fitting the gudgeons into the solid ends of a roller required the services of a mason; David Macarthur in May 1763 spent one day at such an operation, charging 1/3d (15/– Scots, the wage per day of a craftsman of that time).[5] The remaining parts of the frame were usually of wood, both for holding the gudgeons in position and allowing the gardeners to haul the roller about. The strains on the frame called for John Black's assistance over the years, 'mending ye frame' or 'dressing ye frame', with charges ranging from 6d to 1/0d. These repairs usually involved metal 'batts' for strengthening purposes. In May 1732 the frame repairs also involved 'laying two ends with new screws and for a kie for screwing it together'.[6] 'Laying' here means extending; the total cost was 1/–. John Black affords us some more details about a repair in June 1737: '. . . For dressing a fraim of the rowing stone of the physick garden with eiking of the mid-bar and laying on the ends of the cross bar with making a new screw nail with two nutts'.[7] 'Eiking' the mid-bar was increasing its length, and this was combined with repairs to the cross bar at the end by which the roller was hauled. All this cost 1/6d.

George Jarden was the hammerman who took over from John Black, and his repairs (similar to those above) to the rolling stones continued through the 1740s, 1750s and 1760s, with charges ranging between 1/– and 3/–. Jarden rarely left details of his repairs, other than referring to new gudgeons[5] or new washers.[8] Two plumbers, William Pettigrew and Alexander Mathie, were called in in June 1763 to supply lead for a rolling stone,[5] no doubt to help anchor the gudgeons in the stone. In May 1767, Archibald Buchanan, a

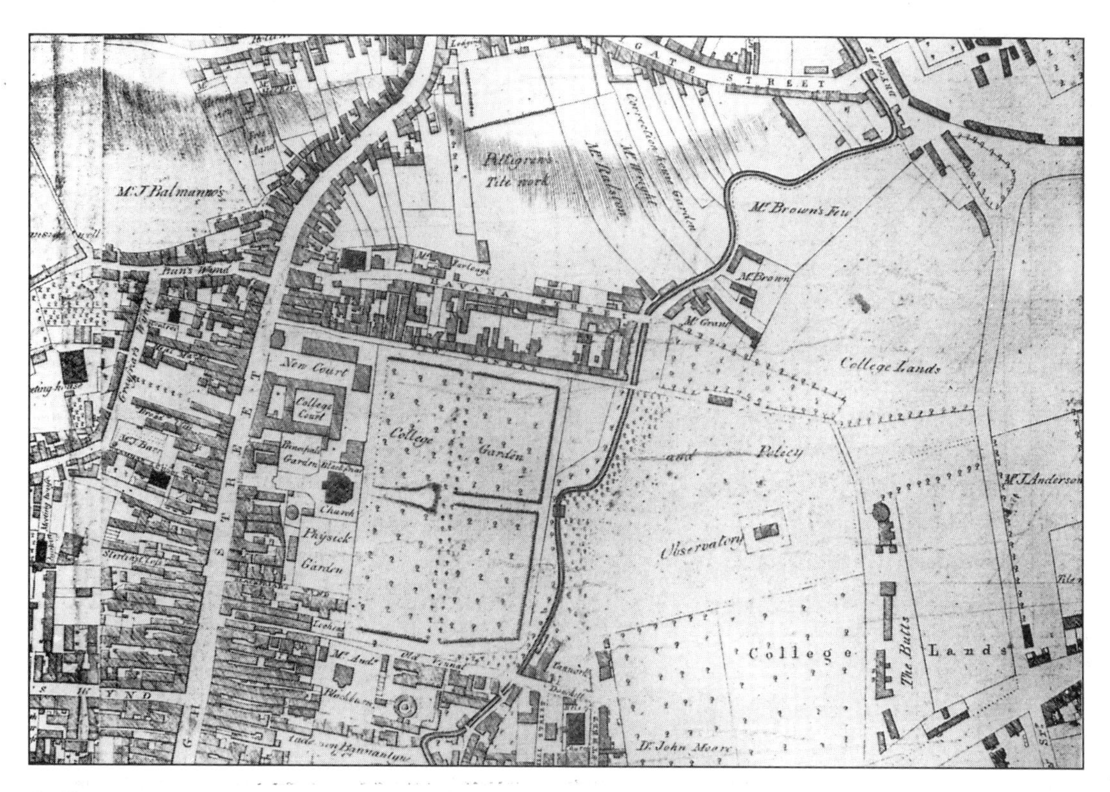

2. From McArthur's map of 1778, showing the 'Old College' buildings and the College or Great Garden. The small Physic Garden lies south of the Blackfriars Church.

wright, charged £1/8/9d '. . . To a frame and furniture for a Horse for the great Rolling Stone for Rolling the Garden'.[9] This marks a noticeable departure by the professors from previous rulings. Fitting a roller with a frame and shafts suggests a larger structure than usual. All rollers in previous years were man-hauled. The professors objected strongly to the use in the gardens of any apparatus which caused ruts or any marking of the walks or the plots, and horse-drawn devices were not permitted. Hence a change of minds seems to have taken place in 1767. Perhaps this roller was the one requiring similar repairs in July 1778: '. . . To work and workmanship with Iron work for a Horse frame for the Great Rolling Stone, College Garden £1/1/9. To a hasp, Padlock and Steeple (= staple) for same 2/11d'.[10]

From the 1770s until the end of the century these roller repairs were shared between John Hood and George Hutcheson. 'Mending the frame' is again a repeated item in their general accounts, though rarely accompanied by any details of the repairs involved. In April 1770 Hood charged 8d for mending the framework of a roller in the Physic Garden, with an additional charge of 10d for a '. . . wrench with 2 heads for taking Do. asunder'.[11] Hutcheson supplied and fixed 'two joint plates for a rolling stone' (cost 2/8d) in May 1790.[12] From all these several account entries it is evident that these heavy stone rollers, hand-hauled over (mainly) the walks, caused repeated strains on the frameworks. These rollings were often the work of casual workmen under the supervision of the resident gardeners. Patrick Stevenson, the gardener, submitted an account in November 1759 which included £5/10/8d 'To mowing and Rolling the walks Six Rounds'.[13] In October 1754 one Daniel Campbell and a soldier from the nearby barracks spent one day 'rolling the walks to sadden them', i.e. to make them firm underfoot.

Wheelbarrows and 'Hurrlbarrows'

Similar repair problems arose with other manhandled structures—the wheelbarrows and the 'hurrlbarrows'. The latter refer to two-wheeled hand carriages as distinct from the wheelbarrows. 'Hurling' was moving a load (soil, dung, lime, branch cuttings, etc.) with such a barrow—hence the payments made to 'hurling men' or 'to a man for hurling . . .'. Two-wheeled hand-carriages are still known as 'hurlies' at the present day. James Johnstone was involved in some necessary repairs, as he recorded in his accounts presented for April–December 1656–May 1658, and May–October 1658.[14] In his first listing 'twa eies & gwgans for ane wheilbarrow and ane pair of old bands mending' was charged at 1/6d, and 'mending ane hwrrlbarrow and ane bucket' cost 1/0d. In the second listing, 'mending the iorn work of 2 wheilbarrows' came to 1/8d, and an identical repair on the third account cost 2/0d. John Gairner, another hammerman, charged 1/6d for 'dressing ane hwrrlbarrow' in 1684.[15] The nature of the iron work repairs are nowhere specified in the above. William Telfer, hammerman, is more explanatory in his repair bills.[16] In December 1718, '. . . shoeing the spindle of a wheelbarrow weighting 11lb 4oz' was charged at the rate of 4d per lb, or 3/9 in all. 'Shoeing' was fitting metal rims to a new spindle, or axle. In March 1719 'mending the trindle (wheel) of a wheelbarrow with a new gugan' cost 8d. In April 1719 this same method of charging for the weight of metal used was applied to '2 gugans and 2 eies for a Hurrlbarrow weighting 5lb 8oz', again at 4d per pound, or 1/10d.

The partnership of Francis Stephenson and Robert Donaldson, wrights, presented their annual account in May 1723. Included was a charge of £1/1/8d '. . . To 4 days of 1 man making a new wheilbarrow, Level and Rake for James Loudon for use in the colledge yeard'.[17] Of this sum, some 4/– or 5/– would have been for labour, the remainder covering materials. James Loudon was the gardener with responsibility for the Great Garden: '. . . one skilled in training and dressing evergreens' according to the University records regarding his appointment in 1722.[18] This same account recorded '. . . 1½ days of a man mending a wheilbarrow and making a new axle tree thereto and shafting a weeding iron for the

Physick Garden' for which the charge was 1/8d. This would just about have covered the wages, so the necessary wood may have been supplied—the University possessed a 'Timber house' somewhere on the site for storage of planks and any other wood reserves. The axle-trees of both the wheelbarrows and the 'hurrlbarrows' feature prominently in the repair lists, as will be shown. These were the wooden axles to which the wheels were fitted. A bottle of 'oyl for the axle-trees of the wheelbarrows' cost 8d. This was probably florence oil, a rich form of olive oil. Mineral oils were not available until well into the next century.

The gudgeons of both wheelbarrows and 'hurrlbarrows' occupied the attention of John Black throughout the 1720s and 1730s. Making a new 'gugan' and 'laying' (repairing) another one for a 'hweilbarrow' was required in December 1725.[19] Two years later he charged for '. . . a gugan and mending the eie wheir the gugan goe of a hwill barriw of the big yeard'.[20] In the same account 'clesping' a wheelbarrow was itemised. 'Clesping' or clasping entailed fitting a metal band. These repairs varied between 4d and 6d. Black described similar repairs to the 'hwrrlbarrows'. 'Shoding the whil of a hwrrlbarrow in the Physick Garden' on 1 March 1727 describes fixing a metal tyre. The charge was by weight—8lb 8oz at 4d per oz. The bill came to 3/1d: 2/10d for the tyre, and 3d 'for making 18 nails for it'. Another charge by weight was made eight days later: '. . . fowr eies and fowr gugans and fowr rings to the new hwrrlbarrow weight 10lb 4oz' (3/5d). Black's difficulties with spelling are seen in an item for May 1727: '. . . for a gwgan and a ring to the ecet trie (axle tree) of a hwrrlbarrow in the big yeard' (1/3d). In June '. . . six eies and six gugans and six rings to the three new hrrlbarrows of the big yeard weighting 17lb 3oz' (5/8d) rather suggest more problems with the new barrows. The above set the general patterns of repairs to the 'hurrlbarrows' over the years. In August 1734 Black presented a lengthy account listing a variety of jobs for the University starting in March 1733. The garden repairs commenced in that same month, viz:[21]

For fower eies to the hwrrlbarrow	2/1d
laying of another eie	2d
fower gugans to the said barrow	1/3d
For making of a new on (one) and laying twa old anes	1d
fower rings to the axeltries of said barrow	1/0d

Later in April 'a large letter C for marking of the hurrlbarrow with' cost 10d. The University was better known locally then as 'Glasgow Colledge'; it would seem that barrows were 'borrowed' on occasions. In June 1734 'fwr sterrups for the bottom of the hurrlbarrows' rather suggest U-shaped springs attached to the undersides, to which the axle-trees would have been fixed. In this same month 'ane new hrrlbarrow' required repairs—'. . . twa gugans twa eies and twa stearrups' (£1/15/0d). One of Black's last entries on the account was for '. . . shoring the wheil with new clamps and 27 stab nails with eiking 9 enches to ane clesp of a hurrlbarrow' (3/4d). With such a sizable annual account as this one the garden repairs played a small part. The greater number of entries on the part of the hammerman was for repairs to locks and keys in various parts of the University's grounds and buildings.

George Jarden took over the barrow repairs in the 1750s. His bills often lack any detail. Repeatedly all that is mentioned is 'iron work for the wheelbarrow'—as on 9 August 1755 when 4/11½d was charged for iron work on three wheelbarrows.[22] In August 1758 '19lb iron work for three wheelbarrows' at 5d per lb was charged at 8/1½d.[23] 'A strap for a hurrlbarrow' in June 1757 cost 3d. An account entry dated June 1770 is more specific: '. . . To ane axtree for a wheelbarrow two rings welded and eyes made straiter' (1/–).[24] This suggests some distortion of the wheel and axle needing repair. John Hood's repairs over the years are given in more detail in his accounts. In April 1770 he listed 'To 2 spindles and kneed caps for 2 wheelbarrows' (5/3d) ('Kneed caps' were metal bands with an angular bend in them), '4 rings for axle-trees of Ditto' (8d), and '4 straps for the bass of the bottom of Do.' cost 2/0d.[25] In August 1783 'laying 2 spindles of wheelbarrows' cost 1/0d,[26] and '. . . a hasp for the trundle (wheel) for ane ditto' 11d. The hasp (or hesp) was a catch or clasp for holding the wheel upright on the axle. In the same account '2 hasps for the bottom of Do.' cost 8d, and a 'kneed plate' was fixed to a wheelbarrow for 4d.

From these several charges it is evident that the most frequent repairs were, not surprisingly, to the wheels, axle-struts and axle-trees—those parts which took the most strain from regular usage. The body works of both types of barrow also called for reinforcements with iron bands, clasps and metal plates. Purchases of new barrows of either type were rarely mentioned. A new wheelbarrow cost 12/6d in 1752, 13/0d in 1772, 12/0d in 1779 and 18/0d in 1801.

Mattocks

The blades and shafts of these implements received a good deal of attention over the years. An early reference is to be found in James Johnstone's account of March-September 1655: '. . . To ane new mattock and mending ane old ane', 5/10d. Of this sum 2/1d covered the cost of the new one. In a later account he records 'To ane new mattock and kyeing and mending ane old ane', 4/0d. 'Kyeing was fastening by means of a 'key' or wedge.[27] John Black in August 1727 supplied '2 big metal wedges' (7d) for two mattocks—wedges to help anchor the blades to the shafts.[20] In June 1731 'laying a mattock for the yeard both ends' (10d) indicates a double-bladed tool.[6] 'Laying' here could mean replenishing the blades. George Jarden over the years charged 1d for 'sharping' a mattock,[24] but 6d-1/0d for 'laying' or 'renewing' one. Again, in February 1780, an unnamed hammerman charged 1/8d 'To laying a mattox both ends for grubbing tries in the Gardine'.[28] One small repair in June 1757 was by 'a smith's lad', who received 2d '. . . For mending the hose of a mattock'.[24] The 'hose' was the socket on the blade into which the shaft was fitted and wedged. Shaft replacement was a frequent necessity. Robert Donaldson, one of a wrights' partnership earlier mentioned, charged 10d in August 1731 for 'Timber work—shafting a mattock and a hammer and mending a wheelbarrow'.[29] One William Anderson in August 1756 presented a bill for 1/0d '. . . for 3 times shafting mattocks at 4d each'.[30] A Deacon Gardiner charged 6d for a shafting in June 1764,[31] and similar charges were made by hammermen in 1766 and 1771; in June 1787 the price had risen to 8d.[32] There are occasional references to the supply of new mattocks. In 1655 one cost 2/1d; in 1754 3/1d; in 1787 3/9 1/2; and in 1798 5/6d. An unusual reference is to be found in a University account for November 1765: '. . . To Dr. Traill what he paid for a mattock taken out of a well in Cartentulloch (Kirkintilloch)—10/6d'. Robert Traill was Professor of Divinity from 1761–75, and seems to have paid rather excessively over the going rate!

Spades and Shovels

The records for these repairs are not always easy to interpret—the hammermen were sometimes not clear whether one or the other was being described. John Black in May 1725 fitted 'two new hosses (shaft sockets) and lugs (shafts) for two speads in the big yeard' for 2/0d. This suggests spades with metal blades.[19] Different repairs were listed in June 1727:[20]

for shewing to new shwls (shovels) to the big years	1/8d
for clesping to two shwls in the big yeard	7d
for shewing and clesping two new shwls in the big/yeard	2/4d

'Shewing' or shoeing refers to fitting a metal edging to a wood blade, later described by George Jarden in June 1753 '. . . To a new shod for a shovel' (10d).[22] 'Clesping' or clasping suggests some metallic interlocking structures, possibly for fitting the metal edgings to the wood blades. This is indicated in some further repairs by Black, viz:

December 1727 'for mending a shwl with 2 clesps'	5d
September 1730[33] 'for ane long shwl iron and clesp'	1/0d
April 1734[7] 'for a long shwl iron and clesping it to ane new shwl'	1/2d

'Long shwl irons' are the edgings at the ends of the wood blades. Metal-bladed shovels were also used, as shown in John Hood's account in May 1780, when he was paid 6d

'To battring broader a shovel for cleaning of the syvers (drains)'.[28] New spades changed little in price over the years:

1721	3/6d
1732	3/4d
1737	3/4d
1753	3/0d
1754	3/2d
1771	4/0d
1782	3/10d
1786	4/0d
1788	4/0d
1803	3/6d

In March 1800 a 'square mouthed shovel for dung' cost 3/6d.

Scythes and Shears

With so much grass, clover, shrubs, trees and hedges to deal with, it is hardly surprising that cutting instruments would have needed frequent repairs and replacements. In July 1706 an unknown hammerman supplied 'a sned and putting on hands and a ring of mounting for a new syth' (2/0d).[34] The 'sned' was the shaft, the 'hands' were the handles for holding, and the 'ring of mounting' the means by which the blade was attached to the shaft. 'Grinding and setting up the syth' cost 7d. John Black carried out numerous unspecified 'syth mendings' between 1720 and 1740, charging between 3d and 6d. Explanations are available in some accounts. In May 1727 'Mending the rwmp of a syth' cost 5d; the 'rwmp' was the blade.[20] In June 1732 two wedges for scythes cost 2d—these were for holding the metal rings to the shaft.[6] In this same account 'a ring to the syth head with a tong (tongue)' cost 3d. The ring and the tongue were probably associated with the blade. George Jarden similarly supplied rings and wedges for scythes over the years, and occasionally fitted 'sneds'. In July 1752 'a syth mounting with 5 rings and a wage' (wedge) was fitted for 1/6d.[35] 'A syth wage' in 1762 was replaced for 2d.[22] 'Sharping' the scythes was rarely the work of hammermen—the gardeners of the workmen were expected to do this with the 'sharping stones' provided. The price of a new scythe remained fairly constant throughout the eighteenth century. In 1721, 2/6d was paid; over the years the prices varied between 2/3d and 2/6d; 2/10d was paid in 1786.

Hedging shears were often sharpened by hammermen. William Telfer charged 2d for 'dressing a pair of Gardene shears for the use of the Physick Garden with a new ring to their shaft' in April 1722.[36] 'Sharping the Gardner's shears' cost 4d in August 1725.[37] John Black replaced 'ane new screw nail to the heading sheirs of the Big Yeard' (3d) in September 1728.[38] 'Mending a pair of headging sheirs' cost 3d in August 1730,[34] and 'mending and grinding' in July 1732 was charged at 6d. George Jarden similarly was involved in 'mending and grinding' shears over the years. An unusual repair in August 1770 was 'to mending the shears for the hand to move in' at 5/0d—a relatively expensive job.[39] New hedging shears were in themselves quite expensive, costing 3/0d in 1724, 4/0d in 1752, and 5/0d in 1756.

General Items

Rakes are mentioned on occasions. The principal repairs were 'for mending the hoss of a reck' (John Black, August 1730, 3d),[34] or, 'fitting ane new hoss to a reck' in July 1732 (6d).[6] As before, the 'hoss' (hose) was the metal socket into which the handle fitted. George Hutcheson in August 1781 charged 10d 'To a new tooth for and mending a rake'.[26] 'Two new Raiks', one of 11 teeth, another of 9, cost 5/0d in 1722.[40] Reels for garden lines received some attention, as with 'Ane iron spindle and an iron pinn to the weel for ane line to the Physick Garden' in May 1707 (10d).[41] John Black in June 1728 charged 3d 'To mending the winch that rows up the line in the yeard,[39] George Jarden supplied 's spinel (spindle) to a Gardners Reel' (6d) in January 1756.[22] In the 1750s a new reel cost 1/6d.[24,31] 'Dutch hows' were repaired by George Hutcheson at various times from 1787–91, 'sharping and dressing' or 'dressing and altering'.[42,43] Patrick Leckie was paid 2/0d in August 1756 'for new bottoming of 2 sives (sieves) the one 10d the other 14d.[31] A new 'Wattring Cann' cost 4/0d in May 1766, and 'mending ane old one', 6d.[44] John Black presented a bill for 2/0d in January 1734, viz., 'A bolt 20 enches long and two eies and a forelock for cripling the ladders together for pruning tress in the Big Yeard'. The 'forelock' was a wedge of iron fixed at the end of a bolt to hold it in place, and 'cripling' was to join together. In June of the same year a 'triangle ladder to the use of the Colledge Gardines at pruning the hedges' was constructed by Ronald Donaldson for 7/4d. The plumbers Pettigrew and Mathie charged 1/6d in July 1772 'To repairing the lead cistern in the Physick Garden, soder and work'.[54]

Finale

Most of the running repairs described are readily recognisable. Noticeably the wheeled implements and the rollers gave most problems. To what extent these repeated repairs to gudgeons, axles, wheels, axle-trees, frame strengtheners, etc, are measures of the quality of metal used is not known—recognition of the importance of metal fatigue is of relatively recent origin. Reference on occasions to repairs on a 'new' barrow is probably more a recognition of the relative age of the implement than reference to a newly purchased one. This same problem of metal quality may apply to the frequent repairs to mattocks and scythes. With both some forcible expression is necessary for their effective usage. It is not always possible to trace through whose accounts these bills were eventually paid—the emphasis is all too often on 'eventually'. In the 1780s and 1790s, however, the gardener, Robert Lang, was allowed £1 annually to cover the costs of repairs to his implements.

For all the care and attention of the eighteenth century and into the nineteenth, no trace of the gardens now remains. Towards the end of the eighteenth century the small Physic Garden steadily declined in fertility, to the extent that in 1803 the University considered buying another site elsewhere in the town, but nothing came of this purchase. The joint actions of the University and the Royal Botanic Institution of Glasgow in 1817 and 1818 led to the laying out of an 8-acre botanic garden in the west of the town, and it was here that William Jackson Hooker taught Botany classes of the University during his tenure of the Regius Chair of Botany from 1820 to 1841. The small Physic Garden was steadily poisoned out of existence by the toxic fumes of the volatile products of tin, lead, antimony and copper from a type foundry built nearby by the University in 1762 and extended over the next two decades.[46] This chronic pollution factor was recognised (and named) by the University in 1803. The Great Garden was less affected by the type foundry fumes, but by the mid-years of the nineteenth century the steady environmental deterioration of the surroundings with horrific slums and factories, which did little to improve the atmosphere, convinced the University authorities that a new site should be found. Eventually in 1870 the University moved to new buildings in then open ground in the west of the city. The buildings and land on the medieval site were sold to a railway company, and all that remained of the prized gardens of the eighteenth century disappeared under railway works and warehouses.

References

GUA: Glasgow University Archives Documents, with the reference number. The documents consist of precepts (receipted bills) and accounts of tradesmen. More than one item of a repair can sometimes be found on the same account.

CA: College Accounts, University of Glasgow, with reference and page numbers.

Faculty Minutes: Minutes of the Faculty (the Governing Body of the University over the period under discussion), with reference and page numbers.

1. A. D. Boney, *The Lost Gardens of Glasgow University* (London 1983, 100–101.
2. Maitland Club, *Munimenta Alme Universitatis Glasguensis*, Vol III, 500.
3. C A 26627, 106.
4. GUA 42604.
5. GUA 58249.
6. GUA 40389.
7. GUA 40659.
8. GUA 58254.
9. GUA 4347.
10. GUA 28756.
11. GUA 58276.

12. GUA 58307.
13. GUA 58244.
14. CA 26627, 177–8, 217, 251.
15. GUA 18744.
16. GUA 42252.
17. GUA 42602.
18. Faculty Minutes 26634, 65.
19. GUA 39836.
20. GUA 39954.
21. GUA 40459.
22. GUA 58259.
23. GUA 58243.
24. GUA 58242.
25. GUA 58261.
26. GUA 55302.
27. CA 26627, 53, 107.
28. GUA 58196.
29. GUA 40660.
30. GUA 58260.
31. GUA 58251.
32. GUA 58304.
33. GUA 40214.
34. A. D. Boney, *op.cit.*, 61.
35. GUA 58257.
36. GUA 42568.
37. A. D. Boney, *op.cit.*, 105.
38. GUA 40062.
39. GUA 58281.
40. GUA 42508.
41. GUA 41514.
42. GUA 58305.
43. GUA 58306.
44. GUA 58252.
45. GUA 58283.
46. A. D. Boney, *op,cit.*, 208, 240.

Scotland's Forgotten Lumberjills

Dorothy I. Kidd

Introduction

Most readers will know of the Women's Land Army but only a few will have heard of the Women's Timber Corps. It all started for me with an article in the 'Craigie Column' of the *Dundee Courier*.

One of my daily duties is to scan newspapers for items relating to the subjects covered by the Scottish Ethnological Archive in the National Museums of Scotland. In the autumn of 1989 the 'Craigie Column' published a piece asking for information on the Women's Timber Corps on behalf of an ex-member of the Corps, presumably trying to find out more about her own history. The article was duly cut out, photocopied and included in the section on civilian life in wartime. During the next few months correspondence on the subject of the Women's Timber Corps carried on, culminating in a reunion held in Perth in September 1990. All this material was recorded in the Archive, but it was only at the beginning of 1991 when we started planning for the displays in the new Museum of Scotland that I took any more specific interest in the Women's Timber Corps.

I was asked to work on warfare in the twentieth century, with particular emphasis on women's role in wartime. When the *Courier* featured an article on the WTC's forthcoming second reunion I contacted one of the organisers, Bonny Macadam, and was very kindly invited along. Thanks to this initial approach I have been able to collect a great deal of material relating to the WTC. The Museum has been given a complete WTC uniform along with a number of items of equipment and original documents; dozens of photographs and archival papers have been copied. I have also recorded three ex-members of the Corps, and several more have sent in their own reminiscences. For the 1992 season at the Scottish Agricultural Museum we mounted a small exhibition on the WTC, both to mark the 50th anniversary of the Corps' formation in 1942 and as a way of thanking all those members who have made it possible to record a piece of history which was well on the way to being forgotten.

The Women's Timber Corps

During the Second World War women were needed to take over the jobs of the men who had gone into the armed forces. Agriculture and forestry in particular had to be kept going to feed the nation and provide essential timber for industry.

In April 1942 the Women's Timber Corps was formed as a distinct branch of the Women's Land Army specialising in timber production. This is how the Corps was remembered in the foreword to a book published shortly after the war:[1]

> It is difficult today to recapture the atmosphere of the first months of 1942 when the idea of the Women's Timber Corps was born. Singapore had fallen; Egypt was threatened; the Armies of Russia had been forced far back from her frontiers; the Battle of the Atlantic was at its height; more and more men were being drafted from industry into the Armed Forces.
>
> Timber is one of the most vital munitions of war, but the manpower available was not sufficient to supply our minimum needs. In this emergency an appeal was made to women to help with home timber production.

1. Ready for work at Shandford Lodge Training Camp with axes and cross-cut saw. SEA 60/16/26A

> Many people would not believe that women could, or would, take the place of men. Experience during the past three years has triumphantly proved how wrong they were.
>
> All honour to the girls who, as volunteers, faced exile from home, the cold and mud of winter, long hours and heavy work, to do a job of first importance for their country.
>
> Here is a memento of their success which all should read.
>
> (signed) Generald Lenanton,
> Director, Home Timber
> Production Department,
> Ministry of Supply.

As the United Kingdom's principal timber-producing area, Scotland provided almost half the 3000 or so women employed nationally. Women from all walks of life, from the age of 17 upwards, volunteered to join the WTC and by the end of 1942 over a thousand Scottish women had done so. After joining they were sent to training centres where they received a month's training in the basics of forestry: felling, snedding, sawing, barking, burning brushwood, measuring, hauling timber, working with horses and driving heavy vehicles. The camp at Shandford Lodge near Brechin in Angus trained about 100 women a month, with some of them being judged competent enough to become trainers themselves.

Those women who stood the course were then sent out to camps, private estates and sawmills throughout Scotland to provide pit props, telegraph poles and railway sleepers for the war effort. A particular feature of life in the Scottish Women's Timber Corps was the purpose-built camps. The isolated nature of many of the forests meant that relatively few women lived in private billets.

Here are some of the women's impressions of life in the Women's Timber Corps:

Joining up

When the war broke out I was in a reserved occupation working in the office of the North British Rubber Co. When Singapore fell there was no rubber so our work came to an end. The office staff were all called up. I wanted to go into the WRNS but all I was offered were Munitions or the Land Army so I told them I did not fancy either. Munitions were noisy and I did not like working with animals and cows etc. They told me they were starting a new section of the Land Army to be called the Women's Timber Corps. Oh, says I, that will be better, trees are alright, so before long I was on my way to the Glen, Innerleithen where I became WTC member No 33 and started on a life that I came to enjoy.

Betty Croll

The uniform

We also had to wear our own clothes and footwear. Of course later we were supplied with boots, dungarees, a milking coat, breeches, shirts and pullovers and great-coat, we wore green berets.

Marie Dick on her first few days at Meikleour Camp in Perthshire

When we went into town the following Saturday we had our full dress uniform, the green beret, great coat, green jumper, breeches (officer's material), the knee length socks, and of course the very good brown shoes. We enjoyed wearing it, and my friend and I certainly were proud of it, and tried our best to look neat and tidy. Both of us bought green ties, and belts to go with it (the WTC dress uniform differed from the Women's Land Army uniform only in the gaberdine instead of corduroy breeches, in the beret instead of a hat, and in the inscriptions on the beret badge, arm band and shoulder piece).

Alison McLure on her first days of training at Shandford Lodge, near Brechin, Angus

Training

The trees were cut very, very near ground level, not as you often see them today, about 2ft above the ground. At the end of the month, we had a test and this was my result! A neatly enough V cut as we were taught, but my trainer's remark "You'd think a mouse had been at it" fell on my ears, and very apt, as I viewed with her the tiny chips of wood lying at the base. Of course the reason for that was, my having little strength as I had

2. Laying in—putting a wedge shape into one side of the tree with the axe, before sawing from the other with the cross-cut saw. The wedge shape ensured that the tree fell away from the two women sawing it down. The lumberjill is wearing her working clothes of dungarees, shirt and heavy leather boots. Note also that her hair is tied in a bandeau, a method recommended as a safety measure to women working in industry during the war. SEA 60/15/12

only been in an office up until then. I had no muscles built up—what a difference at the end of the two years when my muscles became like two bricks!

Alison McLure

I had worked as a shop assistant in Edinburgh, so it was a great change to work outside in the woods. I found the work very hard but after the first week you got used to it. We were shown how to 'lay-in' the trees, then fell them with a cross-cut saw. We also loaded the lorries with the wood.

Nan Smith writing of life in the training camp at Shandford Lodge

One day, watching a [male] driver trying to reverse an articulated lorry up to the sawmill—in fact, waiting to drop a load of bottoming from my tipper lorry—I was heard by Mr Allison to say I could do the thing better! In a way I was sorry I had done so, as from that minute on I was the polewagon driver. I then had to teach some other girls to drive the small vehicles, and also drive timber to several stations, sometimes loads of pitprops and sometimes big timber needed for poles for desert warfare. From the sawmill I took loads of sawn wood, from small to very large planks. Once we got the knack of lifting, we were able to lift weights along with any man, as by that time our muscles were really something.

Bonny Macadam [who had trained as a motor mechanic and obtained her PSV licence before the war]

Camp life

The accommodation was in wooden huts which were very comfortable so long as the wood-burning stove was functioning, but extremely cold as soon as the fire died out. It was round the stove that we dried our wet clothing. I remember

3. Lunchtime in the woods. SEA 60/15/17

there was a loud bang and great fizzing noise beside my bed at 5.30am. This was a bottle of lemonade which I had put there so as not to forget it in the morning. By 7am the whole thing was frozen solid.

Jean Macnaughton's memories of camp life at Meikleour

No flush toilets at that time either although at later camps there were. At Meikleour it was the 'pit', no doors just a piece of sacking, if you heard someone coming along the duckboards you shouted 1, 2 or 3.

Marie Dick on Meikleour Camp

At night we often had to chop wood for the boiler fire and *maybe* there would be hot water in 2 or 3 hours.

Marie Dick on Meikleour Camp

Sometimes on a Saturday we stayed in camp and sharpened the axes. One time we had a lesson in sharpening the cross-cut saws.

Marie Dick

Food

We had made up pieces at breakfast time, and we had a choice of pilchards in tomato sauce, or cheese, or jam and I sent [home] for a drum of malt which I never let anybody know was mine. We used malt extract on our pieces for sweetness, and we stopped from twelve to half past twelve, half an hour for dinner, and the tea was boiled in billy-cans on site (the normal working day was from 8am to 5pm with half an hour for lunch). Somebody made a fire and stuck two or three branches in and hung the billy-can on them. I loved it because I liked smoked tea but some of the girls, poor souls, you can imagine, coming from an office in Edinburgh for her first day in the woods, hands bleeding and heels, very down in the dumps, and she's handed a mug of tea and says 'Oh that's lovely', until she tastes it!

And then we worked on till five and we got our meal at six when we went home. We had really and truly not bad food, it was very plain, in the camp we had a very very capable housekeeper...we went home to sausage and mash, we had soup meat and pudding and tea, or if we had our own [black market] coffee.

Bonny Macadam on life at Shandford Lodge

Sometimes we got a pie and we would put them on a shovel and on the fire to heat, often they tasted of smoke and paraffin, but we were always hungry.

Marie Dick on lunchtime pieces

Entertainment

Sunday night arrived and we were asked to congregate in the beautiful ballroom in the Lodge. Anyhow there we were, the Commandant searching for someone to play the piano and begin a sing-song. Silence reigned! Not a movement until I though someone would get upset if no one volunteered to play or do something! I slowly got to my feet and walked to the piano in the corner, with my heart thudding, I could hear my heels hammering the floor involuntarily, despite the noise of the girls joining in the popular songs of the day. We had quite a night.

Alison McLure on her first few days at Shandford Lodge training camp

Another of my jobs was to convey the girls to Brechin for a dance, or to Kirriemuir, as the buses were only suitable on a Saturday afternoon when we were free. Taking them there was easy, but when it came 'Round up time', trying to collect the correct number that I had taken there, WELL!

Bonny Macadam, trainer

Parades

We had two parades in 1943. The first one was in Edinburgh for the Timber Corps only. Afterwards we had tea at the City Chambers. The other one was for all the Services in Perth on June 5th. We had a Sergeant Major from the Black Watch up at the camp to drill us for the Perth parade. The poor man must have felt like giving up. One of the girls just could not get the hang of it, was out of step each time, but on the day of the parade we were complimented by an Army Officer for our marching and smartness. Another gentleman paid for our tea at the Co-op which was greatly appreciated.

Marie Dick

Conclusion and appeal for information

Most of the women who joined the WTC came from relatively sedentary backgrounds

4. Women's Timber Corps Parade in Perth on 5 June, 1943. Nan Smith is in the centre of the front row. SEA 61/39/32

in towns and cities. When the Corps started to be disbanded from the end of 1945 onwards, the majority were only too glad to return to their peacetime occupations, and perhaps the marriage and children which the war had forced them to postpone. Like the previous generation of women drafted into traditionally male occupations by the Fist World War, however, their wartime experiences gave them feelings of independence and confidence in their own abilities which they might not otherwise have known. This confidence perhaps allowed them to pass onto their own daughters the desire to carry on and reinforce the on going process of gaining equal rights for women which started with the granting of female suffrage in 1918.

Women's contribution to the war effort during both the First and Second World Wars is poorly documented by the National Museums of Scotland. The Scottish Ethnological Archive is particularly keen to build up the collections in this area. If you have any further information on the Women's Timber Corps, or any other area of work in which women were involved which you would like to let us know about, please get in touch.

Acknowledgments

I should like to thank the following for all their help in providing artefacts, documents and information: Betty Croll, Marie Dick, Affleck Gray, Bonny Macadam, Alison McLure, Jean Macnaughton and Nan Smith

References

1. *Meet the Members. A Record of the Timber Corps of the Women's Land Army* (*c* 1945), Ministry of Supply/Women's Land Army Benevolent Fund.

Marriage and Traditions in Fishing Communities

Margaret H. King

This article looks at the way in which marriages were and are celebrated, the accompanying rituals and customs which do or do not survive, and the pattern of marriage in east of Scotland fisher communities from about 1800 until today.

Inter-marriage within fisher communities

It is noted by many authors[1] that fishers generally only married other fishers. Before the days of following the herring fishing, this meant marrying within the same fishing village or a nearby one. This was especially true for the small communities where the whole economy and way of life was solely focused on fishing. The fishing method used demanded a great deal of hard, monotonous, cold, dirty work from the women, who were equal partners with the men in the fishing enterprise.[2]

In the sma-line (long-line) fishing method each day the women had to shell the required number of mussels before using the flesh to bait the hooks on their husband's fishing lines. In Arbroath (Angus), where men each fished with a line of 1,400 hooks, this shelling and baiting took up to nine hours daily—a considerable commitment. Most farming or urban women would not marry a fisherman as it would mean binding yourself to this way of life. In Auchmithie, near Arbroath, if a family had many sons and few daughters, hired help was brought in from other fishing villages such as Usan or Ferryden (also in Angus) to help bait the lines etc. This widened the range of available persons for possible marriage.

A Medical Officer of Health studying the fisherfolk of Burghead on the Moray Firth in 1914–17 noted that 'intensive intermarriage is certainly common and probably is a serious factor in personal health'.[3] In the same report a doctor writing about the small fishing villages of Berwickshire noted that 'to be "a good fisherman's wife" [she] must be fisher and not country bred, and in two villages I know well both mental dullness and pulmonary tuberculosis are noticeable'.[4]

Sma-line fishing was generally carried out from autumn until spring. Many fishermen used a bigger boat to go drift-netting for herring from spring until late autumn. Unlike the demersal fish (haddock and codling) caught daily in the sma-lines, the herring shoals appear off our coasts at different times and places to feed, breed and spawn. The fishermen followed these shoals. Early in the season they went to Shetland, Orkney, and Wick and worked their way down the east coast until they finished about November at Scarborough, Lowestoft or Great Yarmouth. Not only were the fishermen away for a large part of the year but they also needed some of their women to gut, salt and pack the herring in each port. The majority of these women were the younger, unmarried women from the Scottish fishing communities.

This mass movement following the herring was a central feature of Scottish fisher life from about 1840 until the First World War. There was a revival between the Wars but by 1945 it became less common. This intermingling of fishermen and women from all over Scotland led to a bigger choice in marriage partners but weddings were still mainly restricted to fisherfolk. In towns such as Fraserburgh, Aberdeen, Peterhead and Arbroath the fisher community kept itself apart from the other townsfolk, living in a kind of fisher ghetto. A fisher woman who married 'up the toun'—out of the fishing community—was often ostracised by her fisher family. A fisherman marrying a non-fisher was not so much disapproved of, especially if the woman concerned was willing to shell mussels and bait his lines and if they lived within the community.

Since the 1940s the use of line fishing as a method has been declining and fishermen are using other fishing methods which no longer require the manual labour of their wives. This has made it easier for the men to marry non-fisher-bred women.

In many communities today it is still a matter of importance whether or not someone is fisher or not. It is felt by the fishers themselves that they hold different values from non-fishers. Their non-fisher neighbours speak of the clannishness which still exists within the fisher community. From about 1978 on, one Arbroath fisher family known to the author actively discouraged their three sons from becoming fishermen. The eldest and the youngest did become fishermen in the absence of other suitable employment. Both married non-fisher girls. The youngest married in 1989 and his new wife, being non-fisher, could not easily adapt to a life where one week her husband earned a reasonable wage and the next week earned very little, or possibly nothing at all. If the weather prevented his going to sea, she expected him to 'sign on' to receive state benefit that week, but to the fisherman and his family this idea was anathema. This attitude highlights cultural differences that still exist.

Some Arbroath fish merchants inherited good fish selling businesses from their mothers. These mothers, perhaps even subconsciously, built up the businesses to pass on to sons so that they would not have to become fishermen. Today, due to the depressed state of the fish market, some of these men are now urging their sons to get out of fish altogether. Back in 1910 Golspie fishermen were telling their sons to find some other livelihood.[5] This discouragement of sons to go to the fishing is not the case throughout Scotland. In Gamrie (Gardenstown, Banffshire) in the 1980s where the fishing method used still makes fishing a lucrative job, the males are expected 'to leave school as soon as possible and get a good well-paying, secure berth on a boat. The females are expected to get married, have children and remain at home'.[6]

Age at marriage

Peter Anson wrote: 'A fishermen could not be independent until he had a wife and children to help him with his job. He needed sons to go to sea with him if he owned his own boat. If he worked with lines he required healthy hard-working daughters to help their mother gather bait, prepare lines and to sell the fish.'[7] Knipe reinforces this: 'children were economic necessities associated with a labour-intensive form of fishing technology'.[8] In Golspie a father and son did not often go fishing for a living until the boy was of an age to marry because it would take a household apiece to support two at line-fishing.[9]

In the late 1970s the Gourdon (Kincardineshire) harbourmaster attempted to line fish as a bachelor, shelling his own mussels and baiting his own lines. He found that he was not getting enough sleep and was falling asleep at sea. Perhaps because he could not find anyone willing to shell and bait even for payment, he gave up line-fishing.[10]

The Doctor writing about Burghead said: 'the fishermen, as a rule, marry young'.[11] This was not the case in Auchmithie. The 1841–1871 census records show many adult sons and daughters of marriageable age still living in the parental home classed as fishermen and fish sellers. Part of the reason for this may have been a lack of available housing to allow couples to marry younger. Research carried out on the marriage records for the fishing village of Gamrie showed that the average age of marriage has slowly decreased from 1900 when males wed at 28 years of age and females at 25, until the 1970s when males married at 25 and females at 21. In Gamrie around 1900 a man tended to become a fisherman first, then take a wife.[12]

Timing of Weddings

In some fishing villages (for example Cowie, Kincardineshire)[13] Saturday was the favoured day, while in Arbroath and Auchmithie (Angus), Avoch (Ross-shire) and Newhaven (Midlothian) a Friday wedding allowed festivities to last longer than a Saturday wedding when all dancing would have to stop by midnight to keep the Sabbath. One author on Auchmithie said: 'all marriages are celebrated on Friday; and the feasting continues till the following Sunday evening, when the toddy-drinking closes the ceremonial'.[14]

Until the 1930s Gamrie weddings generally took place in December and January since the boats traditionally did not go to sea during these worst months for weather. There would often be more than one wedding a week during these two months. As daylight is so limited at that time of year the wedding festivities made these otherwise dismal months easier to thole.[15] Sometimes two or three weddings were celebrated on the same day in Auchmithie, but this created no difficulty as the whole village was involved anyway and money was saved by having one set of festivities for all three weddings.

The time of year was often influenced by the success or otherwise of the herring season, and weddings often took place in late November or December.[16, 17] In Fraserburgh (Aberdeenshire) in 1871 the registrar noted that as the herring fishing had been successful from July to September, marriages were 80% above the average number, whereas the registrar at Lochgilphead and Tarbert (Argyll) for the same period records that as the herring fishery in the west had been a failure there was not one wedding in these parishes.[18] In the Fishertown of Nairn most weddings took place between fishings, either in the Spring or at Christmas.[19]

An Auchmithie Wedding. Angus District Council Libraries and Museums, Neg no PA 1981 1007 LF.

Handfasting

As it was important that a fisherman's wife should be able to bear him a healthy family, handfasting was an old Scottish custom still common in the eighteenth century which survived longer in fishing communities. Christian Watt of Broadsea, Fraserburgh describes her own experience: 'I entered into a marriage contract at the end of January [1858]. It was a bond of handfast, drawn up by the lawyer. Within a year and a day we could produce evidence of a forthcoming child; or failing, by mutual consent, we could end the contract with no liability.'[20] The pregnant Christian was married to her betrothed in November, 1858 'in the middle of the floor in the ben' of 72 Broadsea.

Unlike the quiet wedding of Christian Watt, for people in many other fishing communities a wedding was the one excuse to relax and have a real celebration with a liturgy of fascinating rituals enacted in the two weeks preceding a wedding. Breach of promise was rare among the fisher people.[21]

Customs associated with Weddings

Partly because of geographical isolation but also through conscious desire, many customs survive in fishing communities which once were prevalent throughout Scotland: the use of by-names, women retaining their maiden names, etc. Many customs associated with courting and marriage may have their roots in pre-Christian rituals which have later been incorporated into Christian traditions.[22]

The Beukin. Although a couple might have been courting for some time (perhaps years), when the fisherman and his father came to seek formal permission from the bride's parents a mock display of displeasure was enacted before the company relaxed and celebrated with food, alcohol and music. Ritually the same words were used in Auchmithie: 'I ken fit y're efter, Y'd better hiv come hindermist foremist. It'll be easier fur ye ti gang oot agin. You'd been better bidin' at hame'.[23] In the same village this always took place on the Friday night two weeks before the wedding ceremony. It was known as 'the Beukin' or 'the Speerin'. The couple then chose a best man and a best maid and a warst (worst) man and a warst maid. These were all friends who would play prominent roles in the following rituals leading up to the wedding day.

The bride and the groom's father visited the manse on the Saturday to inform the minister to read 'The Cries' (proclaim the Banns) on the following Sundays in the parish church. About 1840 in Ferryden, the charge for the Proclamation of Banns was one guinea for one Sunday, 10/– for two and 7/6d for three.[24]

The Biddin. The bridal couple and their helpers (the best and warst men and maids) carried out 'the Biddin' on the Friday a week after the Beukin. Everyone in the village or fishing community was verbally invited to the wedding, usually with the diffident opening 'Ye ken ma eeran?'. If anyone was not at home, an 'X' would be chalked on their doorstep to indicate that they had received a biddin to the forthcoming wedding; in Nairn the bride and groom's initials were chalked instead.[25] Youngsters were sent with 'word o mou' invitations to those outwith the village. A little girl called at the Mains of Auchmithie to issue a biddin to her sister's wedding. She found the farmer and his wife in conversation with the Earl of Northesk so she promptly extended the invitation to him: "A'm here tae bid ye ti ma sister's merrege, an if yer Lordship can be bathered ye can come tae'.[26]

The Wedding Clothes. The wedding dress had to be made or purchased. In Auchmithie this was done on the Tuesday of the week of the wedding. The bride, groom, their mothers and their best and warst men and maids went to Arbroath to buy the dress and many other things. The groom bought 'short goons' (blouses) for the aunts on both sides and for the bridesmaids. The bride bought a Glengarry bonnet and a muffler for her father and future father-in-law and silk napkins (scarves) for the groom's men. The bride and groom also bought each other a gift.[27]

One photograph dated 1895 shows an

Auchmithie bride in white. In Nairn late last century a bride wore a white muslin dress, amber beads and a Paisley shawl,[28] whereas in 1887 a bride there was married in a cinnamon brown dress with a stiff velvet collar, with a jacket-type bodice with a row of buttons down the front and a bustle skirt.[29] For most of last century it was more common to have a gown that would be worn on other occasions. In Cowie a grey or blue woollen dress was common.[30] In Arbroath Museum's collections there is a red and brown woollen Paisley-patterned wedding dress with lace round the neck, dated 1880, from Auchmithie, which was worn with a blue velvet and feathered hat.

The groom wore his best or a new suit, usually navy blue, a lum-hat and a waddin-sark (shirt)—a gift from his bride. The wedding ring and a second ring known as a 'keeper' were bought a few days before the wedding. Both were put on the bride's finger at the service.

The Reddin up the Hoose. The week after the Beukin the best and warst maids performed the Reddin up the Hoose. The house, or part of the house in which the new couple were to stay, had to be scrubbed clean from top to bottom. The walls were whitewashed and every shelf and corner cleaned ready to receive the great store of china and crockery that every bride had long been collecting together. The best and warst men also helped in this task.

The Fillin o the Tick. On the Tuesday evening before a wedding the ritual of the Filling of the Tick took place. Many assembled at the bride's mother's house and after eating salt fish and drinking many toasts the older women went 'ben the hoose' (through to the other room) where the ticking material was brought out and all the women worked hard making pillows, bolsters, and the mattress ready for the bed-making ceremony on the wedding day itself. When they finished, the women rejoined the men, drank more, and sang traditional songs accompanied by the pipes, a fiddle or a melodeon.

The Things. Wednesday was the day of 'the Things'—'the plinisan' (plenishing) or the furnishing for the house. Furniture was received at the groom's home. During the day in the bride's house many female relatives and friends helped washing the 'pigs' (crockery). This was done in huge wooden tubs which were halved hogshead barrels, the same kind of barrel which was used, in Auchmithie, as a kiln in which haddocks were smoked.

The Carrying o the Dishes. On the Thursday the carrying of all those precious dishes and ornaments to the new house was a special part of the marriage ritual. The more baskets there were to carry the length of the village in an almost religious ceremonial procession, the more a bride's heart swelled with pride. A dozen baskets full of crockery was not uncommon. An Auchmithie fisherman's sense of social position and importance was wholly associated with crockery. In some homes hundreds of jugs hung in orderly rows on the wall, and if one of these 'pigs' broke it had to be replaced as soon as possible.[31] Today, in Arbroath, ornaments and china are still avidly collected and form prestige items in many fisher homes.

The bride's eldest aunt went to the new home to receive the china and arrange it on all the shelves. The groom's kist was brought to the new house by the fathers of the bride and groom. The groom also supplied the table, chairs and his fishing gear, but the bride supplied the bed. The bride's kist was brought by the best and warst men. She locked it in front of them and then gave the key to the best man, who then put the key in the pocket nearest to his heart. On arrival at the new home it was sat on the threshold. Thresholds are barriers between the outside world and the domestic sanctuary and were seen as very important. The best man then opened and lifted the kist's lid three times. The old custom was to ask a blessing from the Father, Son and Holy Ghost upon the bride's married life, Christianising a more ancient pagan ceremony of warding off evil spirits, but the invocation had been dispensed with by 1892.[32] The kist was locked again, taken into the house and the key returned to the bride. The kist would contain four pairs of white blankets, two coloured ones, two bolsters, four pillows, sheets, one dozen towels, a tablecloth, kitchen utensils, a 'sheelin blade' for taking the flesh out of mussels for bait, and the bait container called a 'sheelin coug' which, in some places, was a wooden dish, pail or even a syrup tin.[33]

The Feet Washing. On Thursday night this rite of purification of the bride took place in her home. The married women of the village washed the bride's feet with great secrecy and solemnity. After the ceremony a supper was eaten of broth, beef and dumplings followed by the usual drinking, dancing and singing. In other fishing communities, after the bride's ritual feet-washing it was the turn of the bridegroom. His feet were not washed but his friends covered them with soot, grease, ashes and cinders and made coarse gestures and bawdy remarks as they all drank in celebration. This almost parodies the washing of the Apostles' feet by Jesus at the Last Supper which is re-enacted on Maundy Thursday in Catholic countries.[34] Evil spirits are especially vigilant the night before a wedding and the 'stag night' enjoyed by today's young men stems from a protective urge on the eve of the wedding. Stag nights and 'blackenings' can result in severe hangovers next day, so many now take place a week before the wedding.

The Wedding Day. A messenger came to the bride with two leather pouches containing money. These were from the groom and symbolised the fact that the bride was now in charge of the family finances. These pouches hung from a leather waist belt worn below the topmost petticoat. The bride, alone, set out from her home. She gave a silver coin to the first person she met. (In Arbroath about thirty years ago the same old woman always made sure she was out and about when wedding parties were leaving the house!) Then her bridesmaids met her. The groom then came out to find his bride, also giving the first person he met a silver coin. As he met his bride, guns were fired by other male guests to ward off evil spirits. On the processional walk to the place of marriage the best maid took the groom's arm, the bride took the best man, and the warst man and maid followed. The groom did not walk with his bride; this was in order to confuse evil spirits. Best men and maids wore clothes similar to the bridal couple, also to help the confusion.[35] Everyone else in the community fell into protective procession behind. In 1909 in Nairn a printed wedding invitation referred to the procession to the Seamen's Hall, stating in a footnote 'Young couples in strings as usual'.[36]

Place of marriage. In some areas, only the gentry were married in church, particularly as in many remote fishing communities the church was several miles away. Marriages often took place in the bride's home,[37] in the manse, or in a local hall or inn.[38]

It was the custom at Auchmithie to marry in the parish church at St. Vigeans, three miles away. The procession was headed by one of the older women bearing a lucky glass of whisky, and she danced the whole way to the kirk. At traditional stopping points on the journey (for example the gates to Seaton Estate) everyone stopped to drink a dram to help them on their way. They were always accompanied by a fiddler or a piper. It was a merry group which finally reached the kirk and an even merrier one which returned to the village following the simple ceremony. Many fisherfolk in Cowie were Episcopalian and they walked in procession to their kirk in Stonehaven accompanied by a fiddler. A wedding guest would fire an old gun to ward off evil spirits.[39]

At Ferryden couples were married in the manse up the brae at Craig and they returned from the manse in the following processional order: fiddler followed by the bride and best man, followed by the groom and best maid, then the parents of the couple plus everyone else in twos. Coins were scattered for bairns to scramble after or this might come later in the evening when coppers were heated on a shovel and thrown from the window. Many youngsters blistered their hands trying to lift the bawbees. This was known as the 'haisin' in Arbroath.

The Bedmaking. Back at the villages the older female relatives of the bride were bedmaking in the new couple's home. In Auchmithie the eldest aunt (and in other places one of the bride's sisters or another unmarried woman) spread the sheets on the bed amidst much fun and joking. A woman with milk still in her breasts might be asked to arrange the mattress, bolster and pillows and a sixpence might be nailed to the back of the bed for luck.[40] On arrival at the threshold of her new home, a towel was placed over the bride's head and the older women broke bread, shortbread, bannocks or other cakes over her head to ensure that she would always have plenty. Some was also scattered among the crowd. A gun was fired as her right foot touched the doorstep.[41] The blushing bride was then led ben the hoose to remove her wedding clothes and resume her normal fisher clothes.

The gods of the hearth and household had to be appeased. The bride was given tongs to make up her fire; the iron crook (pothook) from the fireplace would be swung round her head three times in the name of the Holy Trinity, and her hand would be thrust deep into the meal kist with the prayer: 'May the Almichty mak this umman a gweed wife'.[42]

The Wedding Feast. At Auchmithie a meaty broth called a 'skink' was served first along with oatmeal bannocks, potatoes, rice puddings, dumplings and much spirits.

Penny Weddings. The cost of weddings was such that everyone contributed either by payment or in kind. These were called 'input waddins' in Orkney. Relatives invited to the wedding meal often gave a sum of money called a 'lavin' (usually half a crown) in Nairn about 1887–1910.[43] In Auchmithie men paid 1/6d and women 1/3d.[44] All who were invited to a Ferryden penny wedding got their dinner for a whole week at a penny each.[45] Penny Weddings were frowned on by many churches. The Mill Street Secession Church in Montrose (Angus), in their 1761 Kirk Session minutes, castigated a certain J.M. for 'attending David Tevedale's marriage publicly, which was a penny wedding and that he was at the feet-washing the night before the marriage day of another wedding . . . The said delinquent had . . . acknowledged the fault of attending penny weddings'.[46]

In Auchmithie before the village hall was built in 1888 there was nowhere large enough to accommodate all the guests. The party was split between different houses with the fiddler or piper providing music outside in the street. He was not paid but collected money in his bonnet for special requests. The street itself was used for the dancing. In other places, for example, Burghead, a barn, hall or a granary might be cleared for a wedding feast and dance.

In 1708 the Kirk Session at Cullen (Banffshire) stated: 'considering that many abuses are committed at penny weddings by a confluence of idle people that gather . . . mainly to hear the musick . . . do hereby enact that whoever . . . shall have pypers att their wedding shall forfeit their pauns [pledges] and that they should not meet in a change hous [tavern] the Sunday after their marriage under the same pain'.[47] These pledges that no rioting or fighting would take place, were half a guinea. If all passed off smoothly the money was returned to the groom the next Sunday. The first attendance of the new couple at church was known as the 'kirkin' and was another excuse for further revelries: again in the 1785 Cullen records it was noted that people were 'meeting together in the publick-houses upon the Lord's Day for what they called kirking feasts, where they sat and drank and gave offence to their Christian neighbours'.[49] In Auchmithie the couple were 'kirked' on the Sunday after the wedding. After the service the guests attended another meal for which they paid.

The Beddin or Hystin. Eventually the rather drunken party then led the bridal couple to their new home to bed them. Some young men usually went ahead to light fires and make pots of tea sometimes containing epsom salts![49] The bride was undressed first, put into bed and handed a bottle of whisky, bread and cheese. Then the groom pulled off one of his stockings, throwing it over his left shoulder into the crowd. Whoever caught it would be the next to marry. He then hauled off his gansey (jersey), took off his breeks and wearing only his 'waddin sark' got into bed with his wife. The doors or curtains to the box bed were closed and the happy, tired pair were left alone. It was said that the first to sleep would be the first to die.

Wedding dances. Dancing was generally popular in fishing communities. If the fishing was bad they danced for luck, if it was good they danced for joy.[50] The first dance after the marriage ceremony was known as the shame-reel or shaimit reel. In Footdee (Aberdeen) they danced this dance on the links. It was danced by the bride and her maids and the groom and his best man. During this dance wedding favours were usually given out. In Nairn all aunts on both sides received new aprons as favours.[51] The Shame Reel is also recorded from Forfarshire about 1860. At Collieston (Aberdeenshire) everyone went to the Forvie Sands to dance an intricate dance called the 'Lang reel of Collieston'. Pairs gradually dropped out until only the bride and groom were left dancing.[52]

In Nairn the wedding dance started with 'The Grand March'. In Auchmithie at 11.45pm on Saturday evening (the second day of wedding festivities) the best man announced that it was time for 'Babbert the Bowster'. The newly-weds headed this final dance and at midnight the order was given to 'douse the glim' and the revelry ceased.

On Sunday, after the couple had been kirked, the final marriage tradition was to break the bridescake and drink toddies in the evening. There was no honeymoon and it was back to the ordinary routine of fisher life on the Monday.

Other wedding superstitions. A mother anxious to see her daughter married would threw her mutch (her white cotton or linen cap) onto the fire as a sacrifice. Sometimes a five shilling bit or other coin was handed down through generations to the first daughter to get married. This was known as a luckpenny. To this day an Arbroath fisher bride should 'walk on silver' (i.e. have a silver coin in her shoe). If a younger sister married before an elder one, the older girl had to wear a green garter or ribbon at the wedding. This custom was not confined to fisherfolk, as in Forfar both elder brothers of a bride wore green ribbons round their legs.[53] A horseshoe might be nailed to the newly-weds' door curved side down so that their luck might never run out.

Marriage today in the fishing communities

People sometimes become self-conscious and embarrassed about carrying out old customs and may even want to deny their roots. A wedding invitation in Nairn in 1914 had a footnote stating 'no procession': cabs and taxis were hired instead to take the bride and the groom to the place of marriage. Since the 1950s in Arbroath fisher folk have not confined themselves to living in their traditional area at the 'Fit o the Toon', and in places like Gamrie have built expensive ranch-type palaces up the hill on the outskirts of the village well away from the harbour area. There are now many more marriages with non-fisher-bred girls. In Arbroath and no doubt most other fishing communities this is still cause for remark but does not mean that the incomer will be ostracised. The non-fisher partner will always be aware that they are not quite the same as the rest of the family.

The rituals described above have survived only in part and are now but a pale reflection of the fortnight's intensive activity and merrymaking. Weddings no longer depend on the fishing seasons but more on the availability of the hotel and church. Most weddings now take place on Saturdays since the boats are in at the weekends, and many more guests, particularly non-fishers, are able to attend.

The rituals relating to marriage today are very similar to those carried out in the non-fisher community. But some traditions still mark a fisher wedding. On the Friday evening before a wedding there is a 'fleg-hingin' (flag hanging). The streets outside the bride and groom's houses are draped with flags, and boats related to either family display decorative flags and bunting. The bride's father gives a bottle of spirits to the skipper of each boat that has marked his daughter's wedding in this way. Strings of flags were put up between the chimneys in the Wemyss area of Fife two days before a wedding, and after the wedding those responsible would come asking for flag money.[54] In Nairn it was the custom to take down one of the flags on the night after the wedding and re-erect it at the home of the girl thought to have started a courtship at the wedding. This was known as a 'lichtie'.[55]

A role reversal has occurred in the feet-washing. The ritual is now called a 'blackening' and concentrates on the groom, although some brides also have to endure the same initiation (for example in the Mearns (Kincardineshire) and Skye). The groom is usually stripped to his underwear and tied to a chair placed on a fish lorry. In Arbroath he is smeared with black grease or boot-polish, and the yellow dye used to colour fish, along with fish guts, is tipped over him; treacle, syrup, and motor oil are used in Gamrie. The groom is then paraded through the streets and left tied to a lamp-post 'up the toun' out of the fishing community. He eventually breaks free and makes his rather obvious way home. Everyone recognises that he is about to be married. Videos have been made of this ceremony in recent years. In Arbroath the male blackening is not confined to the fishers but it seems to be at its most spectacular and public in that community. It occurs in some engineering works and also in the Angus glens. The evening finishes as a male drinking session. For the rest of the population a 'Stag night' of male drinking is the common ritual.

In 1981 a fisher girl from Ferryden was working in Montrose Museum when she was due to be married. It was very important to her that although she was out of her village her work colleagues should give a traditional send-off before her wedding. She was dressed in a lace curtain for a veil and tied to railings outside the museum. A pair of smokies (fish) were hung round her neck and she had to carry a chamber pot full of salt with a little doll in it to ensure she would never want for anything and that she might have children. She also had a notice attached saying 'about to be married'. She was left there for about half an hour. A similar ritual was recorded in 1978 in another north-east fishing village: the bride-to-be had her face blackened, was draped in a lace curtain veil, and was wheeled round the village in a barrow carrying a bouquet made of toilet rolls, accompanied by a girl running ahead ringing a bell.[56]

The fishing methods in use today (trawling, seine-netting, purse-seine netting and shell-fishing) make little or no demands on the wives. The decline in sma-line fishing which required women to take on the role of working partners in the fishing enterprise has created change in our fishing communities. This decline is at least partly due to the fact that women no longer are prepared to carry out the labour-intensive shelling of mussels and baiting of fishing lines, but probably more due to the more intensive, sophisticated newer fishing technologies now in use. In addition to a change of attitudes since the Second World War, fishing communities have become less self-contained, and inter-marriage with non-fishers is more common. However, enough of the distinctiveness of the community remains for it to be remarked on if one does not marry a fisher. The values and culture carried in the fisher community are still held to be important and different from the rest of the local community.

Notes

1. For example P. F. Anson, *Fisher Folk-lore*, London 1965, 55.
2. M.H. King, 'A partnership of equals—Women in Scottish East coast fishing communities', in *Folk Life*, 31 (1992–93), 17–35.
3. Dr. Douglas, referring to Burghead in *Scottish Mothers and Children*, Report of Carnegie U.K. Trust (5 volumes), Dunfermline III (1917), 476.
4. Dr. Calder, *ibid.*, III, 480.
5. N. C. Dorian, *The Tyranny of Tide*, Ann Arbor, U.S.A. 1985, 31.
6. E. Knipe, *Gamrie: An Exploration in cultural Ecology: A Study of Maritime Adaptation in a Scottish Fishing Village*, Richmond U.S.A. 1984, 120.

7. Anson, *op. cit.*, 54.
8. Knipe, *op. cit.*, 120.
9. Dorian, *op. cit.*, 30.
10. M.W. Marshall, *Fishing the Coastal Tradition*, London 1987, 53.
11. Douglas, *op. cit.*, 474.
12. Knipe, *op. cit.*, 117.
13. E. Christie, *The Empty Shore*, Stonehaven 1980, 51.
14. J. B. Salmond, *Silvoceas or the Manners, Customs, Traditions and Superstitions of the Fisherfolks of Scotland*, London, Great Yarmouth and Fraserburgh 1892, 4 (an advertising brochure).
15. Knipe, *op. cit.*, 122.
16. Anon., 'Mairriage days at Auchmithie', in *Arbroath Herald* 1/1/1960
17. J. G. Bertram *et al.* 'The Unappreciated Fisherfolk', in *The International Fisheries Exhibition*, London 1883, 23.
18. A. M. Samuel. *The Herring; its Effect on the History of Britain*, London 1918, 140.
19. M. M. Bochel, *Nairn Fishertown Weddings*, Nairn 1977, 1.
20. D. Fraser, ed., *The Christian Watt Papers*, 2nd ed., Collieston, Aberdeenshire 1988, 67.
21. Christie, *op. cit.*, 51.
22. M. Baker, *Wedding Customs and Folklore*, Newton Abbot 1977.
23. Anon., *op. cit.*, 1/1/1960.
24. D. H. Edwards, *Among the Fisher Folks of Usan and Ferryden*, Brechin 1921, 224.
25. Bochel, *op. cit.*, 3.
26. Salmond, *op cit.*, 4.
27. *Ibid.*, 4.
28. Bochel, *op. cit.*, 1.
29. *Ibid.*, 2.
30. Christie,*op. cit.*, 52.
31. Salmond, *op. cit.*
32. *Ibid.*
33. Anson, *op. cit.*, 58.
34. *Ibid.*, 60.
35. Baker, *op. cit.*, 87.
36. Bochel, *op. cit.*, 12.
37. T. McGowran, *Newhaven-on-Forth, Port of Grace*, Edinburgh 1985, 64.
38. Anson, *op. cit.*, 60.
39. Christie, *op. cit.*, 51.
40. Anson, *op.cit.*, 60.
41. J. B. Salmond, quoted in D. H. Edwards, *op. cit.*, 222.
42. Baker, *op. cit.*, 123.
43. Bochel, *op. cit.*, 6.
44. Salmond, *op. cit.*, 4.
45. Edwards, *op. cit.*, 224.
46. *Ibid.*, 226.
47. Anson, *op. cit.*, 62.
48. *Ibid.*, 62.
49. McGowran,*op. cit.*, 64.
50. Bochel, *op. cit.*, 11.
51. Bochel, *op. cit.*, 4.
52. Anson, *op. cit.*, 65.
53. *Ibid.*, 10.
54. In *The Dundee Courier and Advertiser*, 7/3/1975.
55. In *The Dundee Courier and Advertiser*, 1973, newscutting held in the Scottish Ethnological Archive, National Museums of Scotland, Edinburgh.
56. Bochel, *op. cit.*, 11.

Tradition and Innovation in the Life of a Fisherman's Wife on the Buchan Coast

Gillian Munro

This article discusses some aspects of the life of a fisherman's wife in Gardenstown (Gamrie), Banffshire. The discussion is based on a recording I made in May, 1992 but will elaborate certain points using information gathered in note form during general observation of life in the village. I should explain the circumstances which led to the writing of this article. I have been carrying out field research, living in the small North East fishing village in order to gather information on women's lives for the purposes of a Ph.D thesis. This article should, therefore, be seen as an early and somewhat tentative reflection of the kinds of material I have gathered. It also shows how much valuable information can be gleaned from oral work.

Being jointly supervised by the School of Scottish Studies and the Department of Social Anthropology of Edinburgh University, I have tried in my fieldwork to combine the aims and methods of both departments. I have written down and recorded oral descriptions and reflections upon the patterns and meanings of daily life in the village in times past and present. It has been a real privilege to live and work in a community of people who have received me so warmly and affectionately and who have so trustingly shared with me their own insights into their lives in Gardenstown. My interviewee, Anna, is 25 years old (details correct at the time of the interview). She has two pre-school children: James, ages 3; and Emma, aged 16 months. Anna is native to the village and is married to a fisherman, James, who was brought up in another small fishing village nine miles from Gardenstown.

Anna agrees with the generalisation that there are several major differences in lifestyle between her contemporaries and those of her mother. These major differences include:

1. **Education**: Her parents received all their primary education at the village school on the outskirts of Gardenstown. Very few fisher children went on to the secondary school in Banff, partly through poverty and partly through tradition. Anna, their daughter, attended the same local school, which was by then a primary school only, then she spent four years at Banff Academy along with children from all the surrounding villages and towns. Thus Anna had the opportunity to mix with a large number of children from non-fisher backgrounds.

2. **Courting and marriage**: Although it was fairly common for people of Anna's parents' generation to court in outlying fisher villages and towns (due to the increasing availability of transport), Anna's contemporaries were far more likely to choose a boyfriend or husband from outwith Gardenstown.

3. **Communication**: Many families in the village did not possess a TV until the 1970s and '80s because of their religious beliefs. Anna was in her late teens before her parents allowed a television into the house. Now she and her family watch satellite television.

Cars were relatively scarce among fisherfolk

when Anna's parents were courting but now there is hardly a household in the village without at least one car. The local bus service, once used by mothers going to the nearby shopping towns, is much reduced.

Quotas and time limitations at sea mean that fishermen in the past twenty years have spent more time onshore and therefore they have had a greater opportunity to travel outside their local area. Holidays, which were only coming into vogue in the 1960s, are now an accepted feature of family life. Many of the wealthier families will take two holidays a year—perhaps a skiing holiday at home or abroad for a week in the winter ski season, and a second two-week holiday in the summer, again either choosing to go abroad or to a British destination. It is also common for the family to spend long weekends in their own caravans at sites up to fifty miles away. Less wealthy families will take one major holiday in the year, perhaps travelling abroad or in Great Britain.

If change has been major and rapid in her parents' generation, then it is, and has been, much more so in Anna's generation. Satellite TV is now quite common in the village, particularly in households where there are young people. Also, young people seem to travel to increasingly exotic, foreign resorts for holidays. The younger generation have, or create, more defined leisure time for such activities as aerobics classes, hobby ceramics classes, swimming, walking, horseriding, badminton, sunbathing and so on. Anna's generation shop in distant towns more often than did her parents' generation. Young people buy many sports, leisure and home improvement magazines and so choose to be 'exposed' to a national culture more often.

The increasing volume of new regulations regarding fishing which emanates from the EC and from DAFS has made fishing a more uncertain business enterprise, and this in turn affects the pattern of family and village life, and hence affects the way people see their home locality.

At first I wondered if my 'outsider' role had had the effect upon Anna of undermining her belief in the value of her own lifestyle. Had she told me what she thought I, as a representative of city life and a so-called 'educated' background, would want to hear—that her lifestyle is less valuable to society than mine? But the interview was done after a close friendship of almost twelve months, when we saw each other daily to exercise, eat and discuss! During those twelve months, and subsequent to the interview, Anna has expressed in conversation with me and with others similar, if not the same, attitudes towards her life and the prospect of change as she did in her interview. I do admit responsibility for angling the discussion, and for provoking reaction to certain questions. But I believe that the themes of change, continuity and 'coping' were determined by Anna herself. I have juxtaposed tape extracts from different parts of the interview to make the discussion read more smoothly.

Just about every young man and woman in Gardenstown lives with their parents until they marry and find a house of their own.

GM: Fit did it feel like fin ye left yer man's hoose an at, an ye come straight intil a hoose yersel an he gid awa ti sea?

A: Aye, it wis strange ti start wi cos the hoose wis different, an it didnae feel like hame ti start wi. Bit I wis happy. I wisnae buthert aboot bein on ma own, it didnae buther ma at aa.

GM: Wis ye kinna ready for him bein awa sae muckle?

A: Oh aye, mhm. I wis used til it cos my dad's a fisherman. So at's jist normal ti me, bit lately I've startit thinkin, well, at's nae normal because folk aa aroon ye, like there's mair [? incomers with different lifestyles?] . . . I think, fin ye're younger, ye canna see past the pint o yer nose, ye canna see past here. An fin ye grow aaler an ye look an ye think, 'Well, there's a lot mair ti life than this', an 'Es is nae normal. Normal's bein hame ivery nicht at 5 o'clock' (laughs).

GM: Wid ye like at?

A: I think so. Aye. Bit sayin at, I mean I'm nae .. grummlin or bein discontented thit he's awa sae much, cos I mean ye've got yer freedom thit ye widnae hae if he wis, lik, haein a 9–5 job. I think yer day wid be mair organised thin fit it is jist noo. Cos ye can mair or less please yersel. Ye've jist yersel ti please instead o haein ti please yersel an somebody else! (laughs)

Since the interview was made, Anna's husband had indeed left the fishing, partly because of the uncertain future of the pelagic fishing boats which are having difficulty in getting a competitive price and a market from the East European klondykers; and also partly because of the example set by some incomers and by members of his wife's family who have found work in the oil industry, based in Aberdeen. Although her husband has not yet begun his new job (which involves spending long periods abroad) Anna has already expressed her anxiety and talked of sleepless nights at the prospect of this new routine, which not only affects her but her children too.

Some fishermen and their wives who have infant children have told me that their child has not recognised its father after an absence at sea. Several retired fishermen who are grandfathers have told me that they have spent more time in a few years with their grandchildren than ever they spent with their own children. Anna and James, however, have had a different experience with their children.

GM: Div ye think thit you've got stronger bonds wi yer bairns thin the majority . . . faa's man's comin hame at nicht?

A: No, I widnae think so. It's nae something I've really thocht aboot. I dinna think so cis I mean maist mithers hiv their bairns aa day onywey, so the only difference I wid say is thit they've got their dads at hame as weel as their mams. I dinna think e bond wid be ony stronger. An I dinna think the bonds wid be ony the less wi the dad either becis he's nae there aa the week. Like my bairns—especially James, he's mair for his dad [? than for me?]. Bit I'm the een it's been there aa the time. Bit he still likes his dad best. He ayewis hiz deen. An aye, she's close til im as weel.

GM: Aye, ye'd a thocht thit it wid've caased problems initially, maybe fin they were affa young, they widnae recognise him?

A: Niver. Nae wi my two onywey. Bit fin James wis six month aal, [his father] wis awa for a month solid. An fin he come hame the bairn wis 6 month aal—ken, an bear in mind it's a 5 month aal bairn he'd left . . . I says till im, 'He's nae gin ti recognise ye, he winna tak ti ye'. Bit he did! He wis high as a kite aa that day. He sat in his bouncin cheer, his legs goin . . . He usually hid a nap, ken, in e mornin, an he didnae need een at day, he wis as excited!

What I think Anna does throughout the interview is to try to reconcile traditional attitudes and patterns of life (see her statement about her father being a fisherman) with the stresses and strains of actually being a fisherman's wife in a world where new ideas and different ways of living constantly challenge her, her family and her community. Anna says that she regularly feels stressed, not directly because her husband is a fisherman but indirectly, in that she is basically a one-parent family for long periods of time while he is at sea. I asked Anna if she worries about James while he is at sea.

A: No. I niver worry aboot—butherin aboot things lik at. I spose its wi haein yer dad at e sea, its somethin ye've ayewiz been eest wi. It's somethin ye dinna worry aboot . . . I've nae fears o im bein waashed ower e side or e boat sinkin . . . It niver iver crosses ma mind, nae even fin e wither's coorse.

GM: Fit happens fin ee hear o the likes o the Premier an at, ken? Dis at nae strike a chord?

A: It maks ye think, it maks ye think. Bit—it's somethin ye div mine fae time ti time. I div sometimes think aboot at folk an at. Bit I widnae say it strikes a chord. It's nae somethin it I think'll iver happen ti me. Bit then its like at wi aathing, nae only—I think aabody's like at.

GM: Div ye think aboot it in the sense thit . . . ye wid plan life insurances an at kinna [thing], in case he disnae come back . . .

A: Aye. Bit, aye, there is life insurance

plan[s], bit it's nae because he's a fisherman. It's jist—aabody dee's o something an ye canna be certain. Bit—I niver worry aboot fishin.

GM: Div ye think thit ony o the fisherweemin .. Div ye think thit ony o them suffer stress fae worryin aboot the man? Or div they suffer stress fae bringin up the faimily themsels maybe?

A: I cudnae say I've noticed.. If they div it's hidden. It is, it's hard haein, bringin up two bairns on yer own, aa week, cos ye've .. got aathing ti dee for them an ye've ti discipline them.. Ye're really a single parent aa week, as far as at goes, although ye hinna, like, the ither pressures o money, an things lik at, bit . . . [As] faar as bringin up the bairns, it is hard.

GM: Fin yer hubby's at e sea.. div ye think aboot im?

A: Aye.

GM: Lik ivery day? . . . or ivery oor?

A: Nae ivery oor. Ivery day I think aboot him. If they've been awa for a lang time ye start ti wish thit they were at hame.

GM: Fan div ye miss im maist?

A: Weekends, if he's nae at hame weekends (laughs).

GM: Fit wey div ye think at is?

A: Becis aabody else is hame. An usually they're hame as weel . . . It's normal for them ti be hame maist weekens, so fin they're nae hame . . . it disnae seem right.

GM: Div ye iver feel.. lonely?

A:Oh aye, I feel lonely a lot. Certain time o the day. It depends hoo busy ye've been, ken, that day. If ye're busy, an oot a lot—see a lot o folk. Bit sometimes I feel affa lonely. Bit I dinna ken if at's jist me or if it's becis I've mairriet a fisherman. Bit sayin at, lik fin they're stoppit an he's at hame aa the time [between fishing seasons], I dinna feel lonely (laughs). Nae the same.

GM:Hoo div ye deal wi at?

A:Eat! (laughs). No, well I div . . . I've discovert if ye keep busy, an keep in touch wi freens, an jist keep active, it's nae si bad. It's easier ti thole't. Ye dinna—If ye're busy, if I'm busy, I'm nae lonely. But if I'm stuck in e hoose aa day lang wi the bairns, come supper-time—there's jist a certain time—it jist gets too much, an ye feel lonely an isolatit kine. Sometimes I think it's cos o faar I bide cis it's quaet. Bit I think I wid feel it fariver I wis. I think it's jist boredom an jist, the lack o adults, ken? Company.

GM: Div ye think ither folk see't?

A: I dinna think so, no. I think at's something it you could be the only person ti ken aboot cos you're the een thit's feelin it. Naebody wid iver notice it, it came in cis—it disnae get ma doon. As seen as somebody comes in, the feelin's away! So it's somethin, aye, its somethin I wid say thit aabody hiz thit's on their own, especially weemin thit are here, faa hinna got their faimily here. I think they feel it mair thin I wid.

GM: Fit, lik incomer folk?

A: Well, fin the weemin are incomers bit they're mairriet ti, say, Gamrie loons. An they hinna got, ken, faimily. Well, they hae their in-laas here bit in-laas arenae like yer ain folk. I think they wid feel it mair, especially if they're newly came an they hinna made a lot o freens. I think they wid be a lot lonelier thin fitiver I've felt. It's the kinna thing thit folk seem ti hide. Folk are affa . . . Naebody speaks aboot their feelins here I'na think. Aye, in general. Well, freens wid, ken, confide in een anither. Bit it's nae something thit's spoken aboot . . . I spose its jist natural for maist folk, aaler folk especially—'At's life, at's jist the wey it is'. Naebody thinks aboot it.

Anna's awareness of the extra pressures on women who have married into the village was spurred by a conversation I shared with other local women on the beach in 1991, where an incomer woman had finally unburdened herself to her sister-in-law after years of bottling up her frustration and loneliness. The increasing number of women who are coming to marry and live in the village has, I think, led to this more general awareness of the stresses of living in a new community as a fisherman's wife.

Anna seems to hint in her final analysis above that the traditional way of coping with stress is to tacitly accept that things cannot be otherwise because 'it's just natural'. This is probably why it was a bit of a revelation to hear of an incoming woman's stress, for it made Anna reflect on her own lifestyle. Anna also seems to be inferring that younger people in the village are more likely to question why stress is a necessary part of their way of life.

GM: Div ye feel a hunner per cent capable (laughter) . . . ken, copin wi the bairns an..finances am runnin the hoose?

A: Aye. I feel within masel, I feel capable. Whether I am or no, I'na ken. sometimes I feel—especially as faar's the bairns goes, 'Oh, I'm nae makin a good job o this at aa'. Bit I think, as ye grow aaler, ye get mair confident.

GM: I spose, ye ken, ye've jist ti get on wi't?

A: Aye. It's nae somethin . . . I'd lie back an say, 'I canna dee is'. I widnae . . . say at.

Anna gets her 'support' from the other women of her age who are also fishermen's wives, and from members of her immediate family. They all seem to concentrate their energies and worries on bringing up the children.

GM:How div ye keep in touch wi yer pals . . . if ye've got twa bairns an ye're mairriet?

A: Well, a lot o them are in the same position as fit I am. Their men are at sea so there's time, ken, ti be fulled in. plenty time ti keep in touch wi yer freens. Faaras, if yer man wis at hame aa the time, ye're busier.

GM: So fan div ye see them . . . Div ye phone em or do ye ging an see them..?

A: Aye, phone em, and gang an see them.

GM: Aye, an wid ye meet up..?

A: Aye, lik playgroups an at. Aye, ye see a good lot o folk ere as well.

GM: Fin ye're up at e playgroups an at, fit div ye speak aboot?

A: Oh! (sighs). A lot o different things. I wid say mainly bairns, mainly bairns. An things thit's comin aff ti dee wi the playgroup.

GM: Div ye speak aboot the fishin an at?

A: I dinna, I niver speak aboot the fishin ti ma freens, bit I hiv heard some o the ither mams discussin it, like if their men's awa, discuss the wither an . . . I've heard it said aboot 'the wither is time last year', ken, that kinna things. So the fishin, it is discussed ere. Bit nae intae nae depth.

GM: Dis yer parents an yer relations . . . yer aunts an at, div they gie ye ony help? Or yer in-laas? Div they gie ye kinna practical support like, ken, get things for ye if ye're gin through a hard time? Or phone ye up?

A: Aye, parents div. I'm nae that close ti aunts ti get at kinna thing. I wid say parents an freens are really the maist important, ken, ti me. Aye, they div get things if I need them, an phone up.

GM: Div you help yer mam an yer dad an at? Div ye tik yer mam for runs or shoppin wi ye, or onything lik at?

A: Mhm, aye, I wid say so, aye.

GM: Foo dee ye get, kinna, respite an at? Foo dee ye get a break fae't?

A: Fae the bairns?

GM: Or div ye nae really?

A: I dinna really. I dinna think so becis . . . I see ma mam a lot bit she's workin.. So she canna really . . . she's nae as though she tiks i bairns aff ma haan[s]. I hiv them aa week till James comes hame. Or sometimes ma dad, if he's got time, he'll tak them oot, say maybe for half an oor. At's as faar as it goes. Aye, fin James's at the playschool ye get a break then, an she's in her bed. It's, eh, much appreciated! (laughs).

Anna's circumstances are perhaps slightly different because her mother-in-law is elderly and lives nine miles away; and Anna's mother has paid work whereas most Gardenstown grannies do not and are quite young, having had children when they were young themselves. The grandmother whose husband is usually at sea will have quite a lot of time to spend with her daughter and grandchildren. She often babysits while her daughter goes out visiting a friend or to a sports event. The grandparents may well take the grandchildren to stay overnight, or even for a short holiday. Some young women with children of similar ages will allow a friend's child to stay overnight, even at the age of 3. Young women with families will regularly organise group outings to the local beach, etc. This kind of activity spills over into the weekend when couples will pair up with their children for a day out somewhere. In some senses, then, the women's support network has not changed much through Anna or her mother's generations of women.

Many fishermen now spend longer at home during the year than ever before. Every fisherman I have asked says that he is always loath to leave the comforts of home to go to sea in a fishing boat!

GM: Dis he phone a lot? Wid he phone fin he's awa?

A: Aye, if he wis lik awa the weeken an he'd the chance ti phone. He phones a good lot. He phones ivery day. Sometimes twice a day.

GM: Div ye think he feels lonely?

A: Fin he's awa weekends, he diz. He gets fed up so I spose at's loneliness! (laughs).

GM: Wid he news aboot at ivery weekend kinna thing, fit's been happenin on the boat an the atmosphere?

A: Ye'll get snippets, ken, unless it's onything affa important. Ye'll say,'Oh, hoo did ye get on is week?' He'll say, an it'll niver be mentioned again . . . I think he likes ti come hame an forget aboot it. I mean, it must be hard on him, bein awa aa week an livin.. I mean, he's mair wi at men thin he is at hame, really. So it must be, it must be tough . . . I mean it's affa different here bein a woman, ken. I mean, ye're on yer own aa week an at's—it can be lonely. Bit I mean, I dinna ken fit it feels like ti be a man, awa aa week. I wid imagine it must be awful, ken, stuck on a boat, aa week. Sometimes even langer. Bidin wi certain men thit's on the crew thit maybe ye dinna even like, haein ti suffer at kinna thing. Nae gettin hame a weeken, two days oot o siven, if ye're lucky. At's nae life.

The fisherman's wife's workplace is seen as the home. Cleanliness standards in Gamrie are extraordinarily high. The 'hard work' ethos seems to be as prevalent among the women as it is among the men.

It would seem that those fishermen who spend less time at sea are increasingly likely to help out with housework and childcare, but circumstances vary from couple to couple. Had it been assumed by both Anna and James that he would be the breadwinner and that she ultimately would be responsible for the housework?

A: It wis. Although he did his share o cookin an at ti begin wi. Well, I widnae say share bit he did dee some. He wis awa a good lot ti begin wi, at the sea. So I wis lik on ma own aa the time, so, ken, at wis jist natural thit I did aathin then.

GM: Does James help with the housework?

A: Fin he hiz til, he diz!

GM: If ye're hashed wi the bairns?

A: Aye, he'll . . . hoover.

GM: Wid he dee it automatic?

A: Oh no, I wid need ti say til im, or I'd hiv ti be in a really bad mood an naggin him aa the time. An then he wid tik guilt an dee it then. Bit he widnae dee it oot o habit. . . . My breethir widnae dee it, he wid niver think on deein nithin. He couldnae even mak his ain supper cos he's as eest wi ma mam deein aathing for im thit he thinks at's fit she shid dee. An it's nae fair! Bit he thinks she shid be makin meals ti him, thit she's ayewis, lik . . . Times, she'll say, 'Oh, I'll hiv ti gang awa an mak Calum's supper'. An I'll say, 'Let im dee't himsel'. 'Oh, I canna dee at!' I say, 'Why nae?!' I mean, if he wis in a hoose o his ain, he'd hiv ti dee it. I see a difference because I dinna live ere ony mair. I dinna tik my mam for granted lik I used til, fin I wis bidin ere cis I ken fit she's got ti dee. So I think at's changed, ken, ma attitude as well.. I'na see nithin wrang wi him makin his ain supper or makin theirs an aa, for at maitter. 'Big deal', eh?! (laughs).

Anna told me that her ideas about what a man ought to be capable of in the home have been influenced by what she sees on TV, and also by the fact that her father has always helped his wife with housework (he is an exception to the behaviour of males of his age in the village). Anna intends to bring up her son to take a more active role in what traditionally has been seen as 'women's work'.

GM: Dis James..help wi bringin up i bairns an at?

A: Uhu, aye he diz. He's good wi the bairns.

GM: Fit wid he dee fin he's at hame?

A: He tiks them awa oot waaks.

GM: Diz he wint ti dee at, or div you tell him ti dee't?

A: No, he wints ti dee it. He's ayewis been affa good, especially wi James. He's ayewis teen an interest in his upbringin . . .

GM: Dis he read til im or onything lik at?

A: He diz, aye, he reads things—stories an at til im, an explains. He's a lot o patience wi him, explainin things til im, ken, fin he asks questions, an jist learnin him things.

GM: Dae ye think he misses the bairns?

A: Oh aye, he diz, fin he's awa.

GM: How diz he show at?

A: . . . He jist says he diz. I dinna think he shows it in ony wey, he disnae spile them fin he comes hame, let em aff wi too mu- . . . He's fair.

GM: Div you store up problems? Lik—div you say ti yer bairns, 'Jist you wait til yer father comes hame!'?

A: No, no I dinna . . .

James is a pelagic fisherman. Unlike Anna's father, who is a prawn fisherman, James does not know if he will be home each weekend. This type of unpredictability seems to have had a knock-on effect on Anna and James's eldest child who, Anna constantly complains, will not go to bed at a regular time when he knows his father is at home. Several fishermen have told me that they do not want to be seen as the 'bogey-man' who appears at weekends to discipline his children. So the mother of the child has to cope with discipline problems single-handedly, as the problems occur.

GM: As far as the bairns goes.. div ye think thit you're mair responsible as far as they're concerned?

A: I think so. Well, I dinna feel at fin he's here. It's fifty-fifty then. Or sometimes he gets (laughs), ken, if he tiks em awa . . . ken, he's responsible for em, or else, 'You waatch em ey noo, I'm deein such an such'. Bit . . . fin he's nae here an I'm on ma own, I mean, I'm one hundred per cent responsible for em. Bit fin he's at hame I dinna feel at wey. Lik I'll leave him ti run efter them. I dinna . . . rin efter the bairns, or atten them, lik if they wint a drink or onything lik at, he dis his share o that. It's jist a case o faaiver.. I mean, sometimes they winna hae me giein them it onywey! (laughs). They jist wint their dad!

Ideologically, the women seem to see the fathers as being equally responsible for their children's upbringing, even though in practical terms it is the women who bring up the children. Anna seems to say below that the man's chief role in keeping the family household together is to earn the pay packet—she will do the rest! Thus female and male roles do not seem to have changed much since Anna's mother's days of bringing up a family. Anna has been accustomed to seeing her mother run the financial side of family life and Anna has learned the same attitudes and independence.

GM: D'ye think thit generally he'd be mair concerned wi the financial side, bi worryin aboot makin ends meet..?

A: He diz, he diz worry, bit I mean he disna . . . Apairt fae oot workin, makin i money, at's aa he diz. Ken, as regards financial things. I pey aa the bills, bankin, tik note . . .

GM: Fit aboot insurances an at? Div you hiv ti deal wi aa that?

A: ..Aye, ye mean tikin oot insurance, lik hoose insurance, car insurance? . . . He usually diz at. Em, phones aroon, get e best quote, aa that . . . I wid niver dee at on ma own. At's lik a joint thing. But, lik, if it's ti be renewed or keepin it on, I pey the bills automatically.

GM: Div ye keep a track o fit's in the account? . . .

A: Uhu. Aye, an money it's comin in—aa the money it's earnins [is] written doon. I dee aa that. He sees ti his ain tax, bit sometimes I div as well, lik, he's got ti sign e papers . . . bit if there's mair information ti be—I hiv ti get—an go up ti the accoontant wi't, I dee at

. . . Ye hiv at ti dee a good lot, fin they're awa aa the week. It's difficult if he comes hame on, say, a Seterday, fin aawey's shut, it's jist impossible ti see ti aa that.

Almost every book or article I have read about fishermen's wives has stressed the women's independence and also their dominance over the home, family and husband. What I have found during fieldwork is a combination of attitudes and feelings as to the importance of their lives.

GM: Faa's the strongest in the partnerships in Gamrie, in relationships an at?
A: I wid say men.
GM: Fit wey?
A: The weemin seem ti tik their opinion.
GM: I think thit they're independent during the week. Ye'd think thit they wid learn ti be . . . changin.
A: I think they're independent. Aye. It's hard ti say. I mean you can only gang by . . . fit you think yersel.

The slight contradiction in the above statement is perhaps difficult to explain. The woman regards herself as independent, but this independence is willingly compromised for two days, at the weekend. Many women say they are delighted to have their husbands home at the weekend, but that they are glad to see them go to the fishing on Monday. Anna, like many other men and women in their twenties, now wishes she had gone onto further education, but as a child her parents didn't encourage her at school. Her mother said: 'Oh well, you wis a quine [girl], it didnae maitter'.

GM: I wis gin ti speir ye as weel aboot . . . fit you think aboot weemin's confidence in themsels an aa that kinna thing.
A: Well, I've nae got ony confidence in mysel. I dinna ken if it's wi bidin here.. Fin me an ma breethir were bairns we wer tellt we werenae cliver (laughs) . . . Bit we werenae brought up ti be confident. We wisnae tellt thit we were cliver or bonny . . . I did grow up thinkin thit I wis ugly an thick! (laughs). An niver be nae eese for nithin!

Despite their prowess in household skills and in bringing up children virtually single-handed, Gardenstown women often show a lack of self-confidence, especially in the public sphere. This is probably due to a combination of reasons: the virtual non-existence of paid employment for married (and unmarried) women within a radius of ten miles, the lack of formal educational qualifications; and low cultural expectations of women outside the home and family. However, recently many women have been attending a local further education college to do vocational and non-vocational classes. One young mother told her friends: 'They're affa willin ti help ye. Ken is, they gie ye confidence in yersel'.

How does Anna see her children's future in the village?

A: Well, I widnae like em ti mairry sae young. I'd like em ti stick in at school an mak something o their life.
GM: Fit wid ee like James ti dee, yer loon?
A: Well, I widnae wint him to go ti the fishin. No! (laughs) Definitely not! I'd like him ti stick in at the school.
GM: Fit wey nae the fishin?
A: Becis it's nae a life, (laughs) bein awa aa week an hame weekends.
GM: Fit aboot Emma, fit wid ee like her ti dee?
A: Much i same as James. There'll be nae difference cos she's a quine. She'll be tellt she's got to stick in e same as him, an nae ti be dependent on a man. A feminist! (roars with laughter). Like me! No, no, I jist wint her ti be different . . . I'm nae gin ti push them, I'm gin ti encourage them . . . If they dee nae bad for themsels, that'll be fine for me.
GM: Bit div ye nae worry aboot, well 'If I dee at, they'll probably leave'?
A: I div think aboot at, an I'm gaan ti miss them, bit I dinna wint them ti feel thit their mither his ti be part o their life. I think bairns his a right . . . Ye only get yer bairns ti fiss up, you dinna own yer bairns. My mither disnae hae at attitude, she thinks thit, lik . . . I spose i the aaler generation an at, it

wis a case o the grannies an grandas are part o the graanchildren's lives an their ain faimily, the mams an dads. An aabody sort a, kinna, lives igither, bit aabody shares a life. I ken, I've thocht aboot at an it'll be hard cos its nae something I'm used til . . . I think it, ken, the bairns should hae that right ti mak up their ain mine an nae feel blackmailed inti bidin because they've got ti be there for their mam an dad. I think they hiv ti hae a life o their ain, their ain choice.

GM: Div ye think at so-called kinna 'blackmail' happened wi your generation?

A: Oh definitely, aye.

GM: Aye, I spose it's jist natural ti wint yer bairns near ye.

A: It is. It's jist . . . folk are startin ti think mair. I think an affa lot wis passed doon fae mam ti mam an wis niver questioned, ken fit I mean? It wis jist a case o 'At's i wey it is'. Ye dinna think. At's it'. Bit I dinna think at wey.

(It is interesting to note that Anna considers the mothers to be the shapers of the attitudes of the next generation.)

GM: The village is changin. Div ye think it'll be different in ten years' time?

A: I think so, aye. I think it's changin already wi the young folk.

GM: Fit, their attitudes are changin? . . . Fit div ye think caases at, like?

A: Jist progress, time gin on, mair contact ootside a here. Lookin back, say, fifty eer ago, there must be an affa difference ti fit it is noo. I think aathin's changin though. Aawey, nae only here.

GM: Di ye think [the village] is losin ony kine o identity or onything lik at? Or di ye think it's jist changin, thit it's still the village?

A: I dinna think it's losin nae identity . . . There's a lot o incomers, ken, as weel here, thit there wisnae afore. So at's maybe made a difference ti younger opinions. I'na ken.

GM: Well, fit wid ye like ti see change?

A: Jist the feelin o haein ti be lik aabody else, I think. I think at's i strongest thing there is here . . . Bit amon aabody . . . there's at feelin o aabody's—ye've got ti hae fit aabody else his an ye've got ti be lik aabody, an ye've got ti think lik aabody else. I think at'll may be change.

The community pressures which Anna speaks of—to keep up and to conform—are perhaps what has made the village such a socially and financially successful place, where other villages of similar remoteness from the source of employment have seen the migration of their inhabitants to nearby towns.

To view the above interview extracts as Anna's final statement on the experience of being a fisherman's wife would be a mistake. She is proud to be from Gamrie, expressed best by her conclusion that there is no safer or happier place in which to bring up children. Also, Anna often comments on the physical beauty of her surroundings (she likes to hear me praise them too!). She knows how secure she feels surrounded by family and friends; and she appreciates the amount of freedom she has while her partner is at sea.

To be a successful fisherman you have to be able to 'move with the times', to adapt to new fishing patterns and technology. The village fishermen are renowned for doing just that, and doing it very well. It is no coincidence that the womenfolk are both the carriers of social tradition as well as the movers of family and social innovation and adaptability.

The Salmon Fishings of Strathnaver, 1558–1559

Athol L. Murray

The document printed here could be regarded as complementing the article on the Tay and Earn salmon fishermen in a previous issue of this journal.[1] But its interest should be much wider, for it provides some of the earliest detailed documentation of the actual management of salmon fisheries in Scotland and relates moreover to an area, the north coast of Sutherland, where any form of early documentation is relatively rare. Finally it throws some light on the management of the crown's finances in the mid-sixteenth century.

As regards the crown's finances, exchequer rolls containing accounts of the receipt and, to a lesser extent, expenditure of royal revenues survive from the early fourteenth century onwards. After 1425 these revenues were under the management of two principal officials, the treasurer and the comptroller, whose accounts are extant, with some gaps, from the late fifteenth century onwards. The comptroller managed the crown estates which supplied and financed the royal household. His accounts, however, only deal with his receipts and expenditure in summary form. Day-to-day expenditure in the royal household was covered by a series of household books; other expenses were supported by detailed receipts, bills and other vouchers, few of which now survive.[2]

At the date of the Strathnaver account the comptroller was Bartholomew de Villemore, a Frenchman, who had been appointed by the regent, Mary of Guise, on 1 May 1555. Villemore's period of office saw a change in the format of the comptroller's account from rolls to volumes. Only two of de Villemore's rolls survive, the second of which (1558) is fragmentary. There is thus a gap in the record of the comptroller's expenditure from 1555 to the start of the first volume in November 1559.[3] This gap is partially filled by the earliest surviving vouchers, 68 in all,[4] beginning in March 1558, to which the Strathnaver account belongs.

1558, the year of her daughter's marriage to the Dauphin of France, may be taken as the high point of Mary of Guise's power. The crown revenues provide a rough indicator of the effectiveness of royal administration. When it was strong, the comptroller could draw revenues from the peripheral estates; when it was weak, there could be problems in collecting even from central Scotland. Strathnaver was not only among the most peripheral; it had also come into royal possession most recently. The death of Donald Mackay in 1550 had been followed by the seizure of his lands on the grounds that he had been illegitimate and had died without lawful heirs, thus disinheriting his son Aodh or Y Mackay, who was himself in trouble for associating with the English invaders during the 1540s.[5] By 1556 Mackay's lands were being managed by a chamberlain, John Williamson, who accounted for the revenues in August 1558, though he does not appear to have made any payment to the comptroller.[6]

Williamson did not account for the salmon fishings and nothing seems to have been done about these until the end of March 1558, when Andrew Fyfe was put in charge as 'kinner of the watteris'. Originally a 'kinner' or 'kaner' must have been someone who collected kane (a payment in kind) from tenants; here, however, he was simply a person in charge of a fishery. Confusingly each of the four 'waters'—Farr, Halladale, Hope and Torrisdale—had its own kaner, probably as they had been organised under Mackay ownership. Indeed the account may well reflect existing practices rather than innovations introduced by Fyfe.

Apart from the kaner, each fishing had a 'tutor', a cobleman and two fishers. Unlike the others, the tutors are not named, but their title is probably equivalent to keeper. Each kaner received a daily allowance of 12d during the fishing season, as well as a fixed fee of 30s. The tutors, coblemen and fishers received a cash payment for their 'meit fische', probably in lieu of an allowance of fresh fish, and two bolls of meal, except at Farr, where the tutor and cobleman each got three bolls. John Dempster, 'cobill man and principale fischear' at Hope, had the same daily cash allowance and fee as the kaners, but the only other person receiving such payments was Donald Cowper, who 'servit the haill watteris' in some unspecified capacity and got 12d a day with a fee of 6 merks (£4).

It is clear, however, that Fyfe found the fishings in a run-down condition. He received an advance of £100 from the comptroller, as well as supplies of bear from Orkney, hemp, cork, pitch, salt and barrels. These were delivered to Thurso, whence they were distributed by boat to the four fisheries. While two old cobles could be repaired, two new ones had to be bought, as well as oars for all four. John Wilson, who delivered the old cobles to Fyfe, also handed over five nets, but these appear to have been supplemented or replaced by new ones. The kaners received payments for spinning and weaving the hemp yarn, for ropes to draw the nets, for the float ropes to which cork floats were attached, and for setting up the nets. We are not told how the cobles and nets actually operated, but the method may have been similar to that still used in recent times.[7] It may be noted, however, that while there were only four cobles there were five nets. The extra net was at Farr, which had one for the 'puill' (pool), another for the 'watter mouth'. Fyfe even had to provide new gully knives for gutting the fish. Each fishery had a corfhouse, where the salmon were cured. These had to be repaired and provided with new locks. The repairs were partly paid for in meal, as were repairs to the 'iloch' (not identified) at Farr and Hope.

The fishing season began on 13 September and ended on 15 August at Farr and Torrisdale but on 8 September at Halladale and Hope. Evidently the fish were being cured and packed on the spot, using the salt and barrels provided by the comptroller, at the rate of two firlots of salt per barrel. Quantities of 'hessillis' (hazel wands) had also been supplied to each fishery, perhaps for use as hoops to secure the barrels. A further 60 'cleistis' (? bundles) of them were put on 20 puncheons which Fyfe had received from Henry Mowat and John Wilson, but it is not clear whether these, too, were used for salmon. The fish was taken by boat to Thurso, along with the nets from Farr and the nets and coble from Halladale. At Thurso it was stored in cellars to await collection, a further four barrels of salt being used 'for lekage of the weschell and making of pikill', while it lay 'unressavit be the merchand'. Of the total of 78 1/2 barrels, the comptroller sold 6 lasts (72 barrels, including approximately one barrel of grilse) to William Birnie, a Leith merchant, while Fyfe disposed of the remainder.

Fyfe eventually rendered his account on 1 February 1559. His total expenditure had been £132 1s 6d, of which the comptroller disallowed £20 1s 6d for reasons which are not stated. He was allowed £50 for his fee and 'labouris maid be himself', but £26 was deducted for the salmon which he had sold on his own account[8] and £20 15s for surplus bear which he had also sold. As he had received an advance of £100, the net balance due to him was only £15 15s. He was not charged for the unused hemp, salt and barrels, which presumably went into store for the following year.

It is difficult to determine whether the comptroller made any profit from the transactions. Assuming Birnie paid £4 per barrel, the 72 barrels of salmon would bring in £288. Payments to Fyfe totalled £165 15s net, leaving an apparent profit of £122 5s. But the fishers and others had also received just 40 bolls of bear costing, at 10s per boll, nearly £20. Other unquantified expenditure had been incurred in supplying Fyfe with hemp, salt and barrels. There was also the cost of shipping these to Thurso, as Fyfe had only paid for the onward carriage from Thurso to the fisheries and for bringing the bear across from Orkney. However, as some of Fyfe's expenditure, for instance on the boats and corfhouses, was non-recurring, it would have been reasonable to look forward to a more profitable season in 1559.

Certainly Fyfe was confident enough to take a lease of the fisheries from the comptroller for a fixed rent. We do not know how much this was, as the sum was charged in the lost comptroller's account for the year to November 1559. But 1559 saw a breakdown of royal authority throughout Scotland which allowed Aodh Mackay to move back into his ancestral lands. De Villemore's account for 1559–60, audited on 20 March 1561, shows that £66 13s 4d was remitted to Andrew Fyfe as tacksman of the fishings of Strathnaver 'in compensation for the loss sustained by him through his ejection from the said tack by Y McKy and his accomplices in the year 1559'.[9] This marked the end of the crown's direct involvement with Strathnaver and its fisheries.

Fyfe's account was written on two sheets of paper folded to form a small quarto book of eight pages; the original endorsements on its last page indicate that the present outer cover was a later addition. The handwriting of the text is uniform, but occasional errors suggest that the scribe may have been copying from a draft and at one point (page 5) Fyfe is referred to in the first instead of the third person. The account itself falls into several sections, the first and longest of which is the charge and discharge of money, followed by shorter ones dealing with hemp, salt, bear etc. In accordance with normal practice the account was not totalled before submission. The sums of each page (lateris) and part page (particule) of the discharge of money have been added in a different hand, likewise the unexpended balances (rests) of the various commodities. The front cover bears a separate final calculation of the sums due by and to Fyfe. This is in a different hand from the rest of the text, probably that of a clerk working for a comptroller.

In printing the text the original spelling has been retained with contractions extended, but use of the interchangeable forms of i/j and u/v has been rationalised and the consonant 'yogh' is rendered as y. Roman numerals are given in the form in which they occur, the symbol for half being represented by the fraction 1/2. The main scribe is very sparing in his use of capitals, normally only at the beginning of sentences; the transcript also uses capitals for proper names. As there is no punctuation at all in the original, full points have been inserted where necessary for clarity. The text is printed in its final form, taking in the minor alterations made by the original scribe. Square brackets indicate editorial matter, where there are apparent errors or omissions.

The transcript of the original account in the Scottish Record Office (E.25/1/68) is published by permission of the Keeper of the Records of Scotland.

Notes and References

1. R Leitch, 'Working lives of the Tay and Earn salmon fishermen', in *ROSC* 7 (1991), 67–72.
2. See A. L. Murray, 'Financing the royal household, James V and his comptrollers', in I. B. Cowan and D. Shaw, eds., *The Renaissance and Reformation in Scotland* (Edinburgh 1983), 41–59.
3. *Exchequer Rolls of Scotland (ER)*, 298, xix, 75, 123.
4. Scottish Record Office E.25/1.
5. The complexities of the Mackay succession are dealt with briefly in J. B. Paul. 3d., *The Scots Peerage*, vii (1910), 164–5, and in more detail in I. Grimble, *The Chief of Mackay* (London 1965), 27–34.
6. *ER*, xix, 52–5.
7. R. Leitch, *op. cit.*, 67–8.

8. Fyfe is said to have sold 6 barrels, leaving 1/2 barrel unaccounted for. This appears to be a scribal error, as £26 divided by 6 1/2 would produce a round sum of £4 per barrel.
9. *ER*, xix, 131.

Account of the fishings of Strathnaver 1558 (SRO E.25/1/68) (transcript)

[p.1] The compt of Andro Fyfe kinnar of the watteris of Straithnaver maid at Edinburgh the first day of Februar the yeir of god jm vc fiftie aucht yeiris of his ressait and expensis sen his entre quhilk wes the last day of Marche last bipast unto the dait heirof

The charge of money

In the first he chargis him with ane hundreth pundis money ressavit fra George Monro be ane precept of my lord comptrollaris

Summa patet

The discharge of money

Item in primis for careing and fraucht of aucht lastis barrallis iiij punsionis fyve pyppis full of greit salt and hemp fra the raid of Scrabister to the watter of Thurso xvj*s*
Item for the lossing and bering of the saidis aucht lastis barrallis iiij punsionis and fyve pyppis fra the see to the sellaris xij*s*
Item for iiij pair of guliis [knives] to oppin the fische iiij*s*
Item for four lokkis aucht schillingis to the corfhous durris [viij*s*]
Item to Henrie Sutherland for his boit to carie v chalderis victuale furth of Orknay to the watteris of Straithnaver v *li*
Item for ij cobillis bocht fra Williame Weir viij *li*
Item for ane hundreth nalis to mend twa auld cobillis ij*s* vj*d*
Item for the mending of the corfhouse of Fer xiiij*s*
Item deliverit to Donald Roresoun kannar of the watter of Hoip for the spynning and weving of xiiij stanis of yarne ilk pund thairof extending to iiij*d* Summa iij *li* vj*s* viij*d*
Item for iiij dossane of faldoun [fathom] raippis to draw the nettis with xij*s*
Item for iiij dosane of flote rappis to beir the corkis vj*s*
Item for making and setting of the nett v*s*
Item deliverit to Williame Fyfe kennar of the watter of Fer for spynning and weving of xvij stanis yarne ilk pund thairof extending to iiij*d*
Summa iiij *li*
Item for four dosane of faldoun tydderis to draw the puill xij*s*
Item for xl faldoun of flot raipis vj*s*
Item for setting of the nett v*s*
Lateris xxv *li* xiiij*d*

[p.2] Item to the said Williame Fyfe to furneis the watter mouth of Far xl faddoun of tedderis price thairof x*s*
Item for fourtie faddoun of fleit raipis vj*s*
Item to Donald Reuich for mending of the cobill of Fer iiij*s*
Item deliverit to Mawnis Robsoun kennar of the watter of Torrisdale for the spynnyng of ix stanis yarne and wyffing thairof ilk pund extending to iiij*d* Summa xlviij*s*
Item deliverit for iiij dosand tedderis xij*s*
Item for iiij dosand of flote raipis iiij*s*
Item for the upsetting of the nett v*s*
Item deliverit to Patrik Grote kennar of the watter of Halidaill for the spynning and wyffing of ten stanis yarne iiij *li* ilk pund thairof iiij*d*
Summa liij*s* iiij*d*
Item for iiij dosane tedderis xij*s*
Item for iiij dosane flote raipis iiij*s*
Item for the upsetting of the nett v*s*
Item deliverit to Jhone Dempster cobill man and principale fischear of the watter of Hoip fra the xiij day of Apprile unto the aucht day of September every day xij*d* with xxx*s* for his fee extending in the haill to the soum of viij *li* x*s*
Item deliverit to Donald Roresoun kennar of the said watter of Hoip fra the xiij day of Aprile unto the aucht day of September every day xij*d* with xxx*s* for his fee extending to viij *li* x*s*
Item deliverit to the tutour of the said watter of Hoip for his meit fische and fee xxxij*s*
Item to George Ross for his meit fische and fee xxviij*s*
Item to Rore Canuell[1] for his meit fische xxviij*s*
Item to Mawnis Robsoun kennar of the watter of Torrisdale fra the xiij day of Aprile unto the xv day of August for his expensis every day xij*d* with xxx*s* of fee extending to viij *li* x*s*
Item to the tutour of the said watter for his meit fische xxx*s*
Item to the [*sic*] Tailyeour cobilman for his

meit fische xxviij*s*
Item to Andrew Merchand for his meit fische xxviij*s*
Item to Gillicrist for his meit fische xxviij*s*
Item to William Fyfe kennar of the watter of Fer fra the xiij day of Aprile unto the xv day of August for his expensis every day xij*d* with threttie schillingis for his fe extending in the haill to vij *li* xs
Lateris lj *li* v*s* iiij*d*

[p.3] Item deliverit to the tutour of the said watter of Fer for his fe xl*s*
Item to Donald Fyfe cobilman of the said watter for his meit fische xxxij*s*
Item to Williame Leis for his meit fische xxx*s*
Item to Andro Leis for his meit fische xxviij*s*
Item to Patrik Grote kennar of the said watter of Hallowdale fra the xiij day of Apprile unto the viij day of September for his expensis every day xij*d* with his fe xxx*s* extending to the sowme of viij *li* xs
Item to the tutour of the said watter for his meit fische xxx*s*
Itcm to James Grasych for his meit fische xxviij*s*
Item to William Wylieman for his meit fische xxviij*s*
Item to Jhone Dow for his meit fische xxviij*s*
Item to Donald Cowper that servit the haill watteris fra the xiij day of Apprile unto the aucht day of September for his expensis xij*d* in the day and vj merkis for his fie extending to x *li*
Item deliverit to Thomas Mair for the frauch of his boit that careit ane cobill sextene barrellis greit salt iij pyppis v punsionis ane hundreth hessillis furth of Thurso to the watter of Hoip iiij *li*
With ane boll of meill price thairof xij*s*
Item for the said hundreth hessillis xij*s*
Item for ij airis [oars] to the cobill price iiij*s*
Item deliverit to Henry Sutherland for the carie and frauch of his boit that cariit cobillis nettis xviij barrellis greit salt ij pyppis iiij punsionis twa hundreth hessillis furth of Thurso to the watter of Far iiij *li* vj*s*
Item to twa airis to the cobill price iiij*s*
Item to Paule Williamesoun for the careing and frauch of his boit that careit ane nett vj punsionis ane last of greit salt furth of Thurso to the watter of Torrisdale xl*s*
Item to Jhone Alexandersone for careing and fraucht of his boit that careit ane cobill nett sex barrellis greit salt viij punsionis ane hundreth hessillis fra Thurso to the watter of Hallowdale xl*s*
Item for the said hundreth hessillis xij*s*
Item for iiij airis to the cobillis of the saidis watteris of Torrisdale and Hallowdale viij*s*
Lateris xlv *li* ij*s*

[p4] Item gevin to Williame Rannaldsoun for transporting of the salmond of Hoip and Torrisdale to Thurso in ane boit iiij *li*
Item gevin to Williame Weir for transporting of the salmond of Fer with nettis to Thurso iiij *li*
Item to Paule Williamesoun for transporting of the salmond of Hallowdale with the nettis and cobill to Thurso xl*s*
Item for lossing and careing of the said salmond fra the schoir to the sellaris xiij*s*
Particule x *li* xiij*s*

The charge of hemp

In primis he chargis him with l stanis hemp ressavit fra Henry Mowat and als vij schetis extending to xxj *li* hemp fra Jhone Wilsoun

The discharge thairof

[p.5] Item in primis disponit upoun the fischeing of the watter of Hoip xiiij stanis
Item disponit upoun the fischeing of the watter of Far xiiij stanis
Item disponit upoun the fischeing of the watter of Thorisdale ix stanis
Item disponit upoun the fischeing of Hallowdale xij stanis
Restis ij stane v *li* hemp

The charge of the greit salt

Item he chargis him with lj boll ij firlottis greit salt off the quhilkis I ressavit fra Jhone Wilsoun xj bollis ½ boll and fra Henrie Mowat xl bollis.

The [dis]charge thairof

Item dischargis him with xxxix bollis ane firlot salt disponit in salting and making and paking of vj lastis vj barrellis ½ barrell of salmond fische that is to ilk barrell making and paking ij firlottis salt.
Item with iiij bollis salt for lekage of the weschell and making of pikill sa lang as the fische lay in Thurso unressavit be the merchand.

Restis viij b ij f salt

[p.6] The charge of barrellis pypis and punscheonis
In primis he chargis him with viij last barrellis v pypis ressavit fra Henrie Mowat and als with xx punscheonis ressavit fra Jhone Wilsoun xvj and fra Henrie Mowat iiij.

The discharge thairof

Item he dischargis him of sex lastis and sex barrellis and half ane barrell of the saidis barrellis in the quhilkis the salmond of the saidis watteris wes put.
Restis j last v barrellis 1/2 barrell

The charge of beir

In primis he chargis him with v chalderis bere ressavit fra Maister Williame Mudy be ane precept of my lord comptrollaris.
Summa patet

The discharge thairof

Item he dischargis him of twa bollis beir gevin to the tutour of the watter of Hoip for his expensis Item of ij bollis beir gevin to George Roiss fischear of the said watter to his expensis. Item of ij bollis beir gevin to Rore Canuel ane uther of the fischearis of the said watter. Item deliverit to Thormot Makanemoir and William Mcanemoir for bigging of the corfhous and halding up of the iloch[?] twa bollis j firlot beir. Item of ij bollis beir deliverit to the tutour of the watter of Torrisdale. Item of ij bollis beir deliverit to Tailyeour cobilman of the said watter

[p.7] Item of twa bollis beir deliverit to Andro Merchand ane of the fischearis of the said watter. Item of ij bollis beir deliverit to Gilliecrist tutour [? fischear] of the said water. Item of j[2] bollis beir deliverit to Williame [? and] Jhone Robsoun for uphalding and making of the corfhouse of Torrisdale. Item of iij bollis beir deliverit to the tutour of the watter of Far. Item of iij bollis beir deliverit to the cobilman of the said watter. Item of ij bollis beir deliverit to Williame Leis ane of the fischearis of the said watter and als of ij bollis beir deliverit to Andro Leis ane uther of the fischearis of the said watter. Item of j boll beir for the uphalding of the iloch of Poldgalyeing. Item of ane boll beir for the uphalding of the corfhous of Far. Item of ij bollis beir deliverit to the tutour of the watter of Hallowdale. Item of ij bollis beir deliverit to James Grasych ane of the fischearis of the said watter. Item of ij bollis beir and ane half deliverit to William Wyliman ane of the fischearis and cobilmen of the said watter. Item of ij bollis beir deliverit to Jhone Dow ane uther of the fischearis of the said watter. Item of ij bolis beir deliverit for the biging and uphalding of the corfhous of the said watter to Williame Moir and all the victuale abone writtin gevin to the saidis fischearis for the making of thair expensis.
Summa ij c vij b iij f
Restis ij c viij b j f

The charge of the pyk [pitch]

Item he chargis him with ane barrell of pik ressavit fra Henrie Mowat. The quhilk the said comptar hes disponit the samyn upoun the piking and graything of the four cobillis of the watteris of Hoip Far Torrisdale and Hallowdale.

Item he chargis him with lx cleistis of hessillis quhilkis the said comptar hes causit put upoun the saidis xx punscheionis.

Item he chargis him with thre stane corkis ressavit fra Henrie Mowat quhilkis ar spendit and disponit upoun the fyve nettis of the saidis watteris.

[p.8] The chargis of the cobillis and nettis

Item coft be him self ij cobillis
Item ressavit fra Jhone Wilsoun ij cobillis
Item ressavit fra Jhone Wilsoun fyve nettis.

The charge of the salmond

Item ressavit of the haill fischeingis of Strathnaver sen his entre thairto vj lastis vj barrellis half barrell. Off the quhilkis he deliverit at the comptrollaris command to Williame Berny in Leith sex lastis salmond and thairof ane last of girlsis or thairby.
Et sua restis vj b salmont[3]

[Endorsements on p.8]
Androw Fiff compt 1558
Compt off the fisching of Stranaver anno 1559 [*sic*]
jcxxxij *li* xviij*d*

[Added on front cover]
The [fischingis of Strana]wair 1558 maid be [Androw Fiff][4]

In primis be his compt buk he hes spendit upoun the saidis fischingis in mone as the said compt beris jcxxxij *li* xviij*d* Off the quhilk my lord comptrollar deducis for certane unrationable allocationis and expensis he allegis he maid quhilk is nocht to be allowit xx *li* xviij*d*.
Et sic restis jcxij *li*. Of the quhilk he hes rasavit fra George Munro jc *lib*. Et sic restis awand to him xij *li*.

Mare the said Androw suld haif for his fe and labouris maid be hym selff at the saidis fischingis fifty *lib*.
And sua thair wilbe awand to the said Androw in the haill lxij *li*. Off the quhilk thair is to be deducit for vj barrellis salmont sauld be hym of the salmont of the saidis watteris at xxvj *li*. Mair he is awand fourty bollis j f beir of Orknay rasavit be hym fra the chalmerlain atour the beir that he spendit upoun the said fisching and fischaris at xs the boll. Summa xx li vs. Et sua restis awand to the said Androw all maner of thingis deducit and allowit xv li xvs

[Endorsed on back cover]
Comptis of the fischingis of Stranaver 1558

Notes

1. Reading uncertain. The third letter is abbreviated and could be m or n; the fourth letter could be n or u. Occurs again (unabbreviated) on p.6, where the third letter appears to be n but the remainder is partly illegible. The name is probably Canwell (G. F. Black, *The Surnames of Scotland*, 132).
2. Altered from ‘ij’.
3. There is an error of 1/2 barrel.
4. Heading partly torn away.

Some Decorated Curling Stones

David B. Smith

The game of curling was played widely throughout Lowland Scotland in the eighteenth century.[1] Until the last quarter, natural boulders, or channel stones, were favoured. There was little skill involved in the making of such a stone beyond its selection from the bed of the river, as the minutes of Blairgowrie Curling Society show.[2] The running surface might be dressed smooth by a mason, or some egregious irregularities cloured away, but beyond the leading in of an iron handle the stones were used practically in the state of nature.

By the end of the century it became apparent that a stone of circular shape would add immeasurably to the pleasure of the game, by involving science and precision, for the course of a stone, after it struck another, would no longer depend on chance, but could be predicted. By about 1820 channel stones had had their day.

It is scarcely hyperbole to state that curling underwent an explosion of popularity from that time. Clubs sprang up in nearly every parish. A national club, designed to incorporate and guide all the local clubs, was formed in 1838. There were 42 member clubs at its inception, but by the 1880s the number was about 600, and every Scottish county had at least one curling club affiliated to the national body, the Royal Caledonian Curling Club.

Who made the curling stones? The answer is not easy, for until the 1860s we have no notices of professional curling-stone makers.[3]

It is clear that in the earlier decades local masons—a trade that abounded—turned their hands to supplying curlers' needs. Most of them remain anonymous: a single name survives from the eighteenth century. William Grierson, a young merchant from Dumfries, left a diary in which he made remarks about his daily doings from 1790 until 1809. The diary was edited and published in 1980 by John Davies of Penpont, under the title of *Apostle to Burns: The Diaries of William Grierson*. In his entry for 24 January 1795 we find the first reference to a named curling stone maker:

> About 11'oclock went to the river and played at the curling all day, having got a new stone from T. Grier mason, Penpont. There was 16 of us playing, 8 on each side. The side that I was on gained. We played for 2d a game. At 7 o'clock went to W Bryden's to drink the winnings.[4]

In many parts of Scotland until the late 1850s the game did not require pairs of stones, for rinks of curlers consisted of from seven to nine men each playing a single stone.

Most of the early circular stones were unsophisticated, utilitarian objects of what is known as the single-soled variety; that is, the handle was permanently fixed to the upper surface of the stone, so that it could run only on its lower surface, or sole. (The design of stone which is now universal comprises a handle, affixed to a bolt, located in a hole drilled through the centre of the stone, so that by unscrewing the handle and reversing the stone, a player can use both sides of it as running surfaces.)

Although single-soled stones varied greatly in size and profile—some being squarish and dumpy in cross-section, some being wide and flattish, and others being pleasantly rounded—nearly every one had a perfectly flat top surface. Most such stones were plain, but a small proportion had some decoration.

1. Whin, roughly dressed, with the initials, 'TT' carved on the top surface, perhaps *c.*1802. The stone comes from Duddingston, and Thomas Trotter was one of the early members of the Duddingston Curling Society, founded in 1795. He joined in 1802, and was then latterly a captain in the 10th Militia. *Author's Collection.*

2. This stone of early nineteenth-century date was found in a derelict cottage in Crossmichael, Ayrshire. It bears the inscription 'Thos McGill'. *Author's Collection.*

3. Stone with painted decoration, *c.*1845, Kilmarnock. One of a pair owned by Charles Aird, tailor, who was a member of Kilmarnock Townend Curling Club from 1842 to 1897. Such stones were still in use in Kilmarnock in the 1890s. *Dick Institute, Kilmarnock.*

The commonest form of decoration for this surface consisted in the strictly utilitarian addition of either the initials (Fig. 1) or name (Fig. 2) of the owner. Such stones were not uncommon.[5] It may be that painted decoration was as common, but very few painted stones have survived in their original condition (Fig. 3).

Although the flat upper surface might be thought of as ideal for more elaborate incised decoration, the number of stones so decorated is very small. No doubt the additional expense was a major reason why this was not done, for even a plain curling stone was a fairly expensive 'plaything'. (In 1845 Paisley St Mirren Curling club ordered five pairs of stones of a weight of 30 to 34 lbs from an Auchinleck mason at a price of four pence per pound.[6] That is, each stone cost from ten to eleven shillings, and that at a time when a labourer earned about one shilling and sixpence a day in winter and two shillings in summer, and a skilled artisan three or four shillings).

Elaborate decoration would add appreciably to the hours of masonic labour and thus to the cost of a stone. Some decoration was comparatively simple, as, for example, a star (Fig. 4). On some stones the decoration took the form of appropriate insignia, such as the mason's square and dividers (Fig. 5). On others there were stylised flowers (Fig. 6). Figure 7 is an example of very highly finished decoration. It appears that the whole top half of the stone was finished and polished before the very sophisticated star was made by cutting away the polished surface around it, and the very unusual scalloped edge above the striking band was created in the same way. (In most scalloped stones the scalloped edge faces 'icewards'.) (Fig. 8).

Two elaborately decorated stones that come from Dumfriesshire merit special mention.

The first, from Eskdale near Langholm, is made of dark, fine-grained whinstone. Round the edge of the top surface are incised in fairly shallow carving two stalks of thistle, each with leaves and flowers. The pattern can be seen without difficulty but I have used chalk to enhance the appearance for the camera (Fig. 9).

The second of these stones was dug up in the garden of Cairnmill, a house on the margin of the village of Penpont, and is therefore almost certainly of local manufacture (Fig. 10). The game was played in that parish and the surrounding parishes in the eighteenth century.

The mason's design fills the whole upper surface, the initials of the owner, 'E H', are elegantly cut in the centre, placed on each side of a stylised floret; and round the edge, emerging from a voluptuously tied bow, are delicately incised stems bearing in profusion a stylised wild flower, which looks very like heartsease, or wild pansy. In addition, on a narrow rounded shoulder of the stone is a band of what can best be described as stylised foliage; and the decoration is completed with a band of scalloped edging. In all, it is quite the most decorated stone that I have hitherto seen. It is unfortunate that the carver has chosed to exercise his skill on a most unsuitable surface, for the stone is of a course grain and speckled appearance; and it is only in certain lighting that the design can be at all easily discerned. In fact, when I first saw the stone I could not make out the flowers which the owner said were there. I wonder, therefore, whether the original conception included picking out the shallow pattern with gilding or other pigment; although, if that were so, no trace of it now remains.

The skill and craftsmanship bestowed upon these humble implements of 'Scotia's ancient, manly game' in a very poignant way demonstrate the regard in which the game was held by its devotees.

Acknowledgment: all photographs are by Ian MacKenzie, School of Scottish Studies.

Notes

1. See J. Kerr, *History of Curling*, Edinburgh 1890, chapter 4, and D. B. Smith, *Curling: An Illustrated History*, Edinburgh 1981, 8–34.
2. Minute Book of Blairgowrie Curling Society, quoted in Smith, *op. cit.*, 42–44.
3. The present writer has recently been privileged to borrow a MS Account Book

4. Reddish stone, *c.*1850, decorated with a crudely incised star, perhaps from Dalmellington, Ayrshire. *Author's Collection.*

5. Reddish brown stone, *c.*1850, decorated with a mason's square and dividers. from Selkirk. *Author's Collection.*

6. Brown stone *c.*1850, decorated with stylised flower. Provenance unknown. *Author's Collection.*

7. Whin, *c.*1850, decorated with star and scalloped edge. Corsock, Kirkcudbrightshire. *Author's Collection.*

8. Whin, *c.*1850, decorated with scalloped edge. Only the upright part of the handle is original. It is of cast brass. The grip of the handle is a modern reconstruction. Castle Douglas, Kirkcudbrightshire. *Author's Collection.*

9. Whin, *c.*1850, decorated with thistles. Eskdale, Dumfriesshire. *Author's Collection.*

10. Greyish-green speckled stone, *c*.1850. Dug up in the garden of John Davies at Penpont, Dumfriesshire, and given to the author. It was this donation which prompted this note. *Author's Collection*.

of a curling-stone maker who operated in Barbieston, Ayrshire, from at least 1861 until 1889. This book appears to be the only surviving record of curling-stone manufacture from the nineteenth century. It is the present writer's intention to publish some account of its contents. In 1865 a pair of his cheapest stones cost 24 shillings, without handles. In that year his two workmen were paid 2 shillings per day.

4. At p.31.
5. For other examples see Kerr, *op. cit.*, 63, and Smith, *op. cit.*, 37, 39.
6. From the Minute Book of the club in the custody of the club.

Shorter Notes

The Scottish Herring Market and the Finkelsteins

George Bruce

In *ROSC* 3 (1987), 111–114, some notes were published on Scottish Herring Markets in the Baltic and Russia, based on information about the Finkelstein family. Peterhead and Fraserburgh were amongst their business bases. Further information about them has been supplied by Dr George Bruce, poet and broadcaster, whose Fraserburgh family had business dealings with the Finkelsteins. He writes as follows:

I respond to your query about the Finkelsteins. Bear in mind that my recollections are from over 75 years ago about Abram Finkelstein. The memories come to me as vivid impressions, important to me in their giving the sensation of a style of life—and I use style in its meaning of stylish as well as cultural connotation. Just how strong is the effect of the word 'Finkelstein' in my consciousness may be gathered from the slight shock I felt when for the first time minutes ago (on reading the notes in *ROSC* 3) I learned there was such a person as a Harry Finkelstein. To me as a child, but also to my mother at least, the tribe as represented by Abram—though here I pause for I knew him only as 'Mr'—came from a far country, who conducted their affairs with dignity and politeness, a politeness which was reciprocated in my father's business dealings with Mr Finkelstein and, for that matter with other Jews such as Mr Stern and Mr Diamendstein, but these were names to me only, whereas I had shaken hands with Mr Finkelstein. To me, a child, he represented the dignity and formality of the race, a concept confirmed years later when Mr Finkelstein brought with him to Fraserburgh his niece, Naomi. Beautiful, dark-haired Naomi—she must have been about twelve but she looked older and I about to become a student—recited poems by Walter de la Mare to me, and I had already been entranced by such poems as his mysterious *The Listeners*. Now you will begin to appreciate why I felt a little nonplussed at the introduction of the warm, chummy name Harry into the company of names and of people whose behaviour related to the civilised implication of the names. But my impression as a child was based on a particular experience, a prelude to a business deal, which may have occurred many times, but at which I was present once only, and which was my first meeting with Mr Finkelstein.

The episode began with a phone call from my father, who was in his office, to my mother. I overheard her say 'yes' to his query, which was, she explained to me, 'Was the piano ready for Mr Finkelstein?' She also told me that he would be playing Chopin. I was too young to think this custom was in any way peculiar. In any case the Winkelmann piano had resounded in my ears with music mainly by Beethoven many times, the pianist being my Aunty Vi, my father's sister, an acknowledged accomplished pianist. By the time I was eleven years old I must have heard her play the great majority of Beethoven sonatas. On these occasions I was her only listener for she would arrive on a Saturday morning when I was about, and from the age of five found the music overpoweringly attractive. The piano at which Mr Finkelstein was to sit was in frequent use. At the musical evenings I could overhear from outside the drawingroom door Bach and Handel sung by my mother and her sister Jessie. On the walls were paintings by my mother, Uncle Charles and others. So the elegant room was not a stranger to international arts, nor had their practice begun in my parents' generation. George Reid, later Sir George Reid, PRSA, stayed with my grandfather, and went on painting expeditions with my Uncle Charles. In any case such was Mr Finkelstein's impact that I remember the shade of his grey suit to this day.

It was George Bruce, my grandfather, who had won the respect of business men from the continent, which continued in the next generation. A matter of weeks after I had been appointed to the post of BBC producer in Aberdeen I was stopped in Union Street by the Provost of Fraserburgh who was accompanied by the Aberdeen Town Clerk—the date was early 1947. The Provost said: 'This man's grandfather introduced the trade to the Baltic'. I have in my possession two silver spoons with the word Pernau engraved on them and the date 1815. I think my grandfather's journeys were in the latter part of the 19th century. I cannot tell at what point the trading through the Finkelsteins began, but it continued with the Baltic ports until the demise of the firm in 1941. When John Speirs was appointed a lecturer in English Literature at the University of Riga in 1934 or '35 he was greatly heartened by seeing as he got off the ship a number of barrels with the words 'A Bruce & Co' stamped on them.

There was, then, a community of interest beyond business between the Bruces and the Jews, but the foundation of the relationship was mutual trust. Of course there were variables in the relationships—my father preferred to deal with Abram rather than Leon Finkelstein. The final test of honesty, however, came to Mr Stern. Over the phone in Fraserburgh—Mr Stern was in the Bellslea Hotel—my father did a deal involving at least a thousand pounds (the date about 1926). The next morning, as my father put it 'the bottom fell out of the market'. I overheard him say to my mother: 'That's the end of that'. He was wrong; Mr Stern's word was as good as his bond, as was my father's for that matter. The deal stood.

Footnote

George Bruce contributed an article on 'Nearly always summer, Some notes from a childhood in the port of Fraserburgh', to *Scottish International* No 2, 1968. Part of it is reproduced here because it adds life to the way in which business was then conducted:

Mr Finkelstein, large to my eyes, in a light grey suit, walked between the rows of up-ended barrels on the bright summer day. He fitted the suit perfectly. Behind him walked a small man in an ill-fitting suit. Behind these two a strong man with an adze in his big right hand and behind him a boy carrying a basin of water. Over the boy's forearm was a hand towel. Mr Finkelstein stops and points to one of the barrels. The cooper knock off the hoop securing the wooden end of the barrel and then with a single blow displaces the end, which he then removes. Mr Finkelstein plunges a hand into the barrel, withdraws a herring, feels it, scrutinises it and then bites it. He drops the fish on the ground, dips his hand in the water and the procession proceeds on its way until Mr Finkelstein halts to make another random choice. On the basis of the appearance, feel and taste of the herring he will made a deal for perhaps a thousand barrels, nine hundred herring to the barrel or so, with the small man, my father. The deal will be concluded in an office so shabby and pokey that the Income Tax inspector could not believe this was the headquarters of the oldest and one of the largest herring curing firms in Britain. But the ritual began earlier when my father phoned my mother to say that Mr Finkelstein was on his way to the house to play our piano.

Medieval Bread in Scotland

Nicholas Mayhew

Since 1985 I have been involved in a research project devoted to medieval Scottish prices.[1] The obstacles to such work are numerous and well known, and may account for the fact that no such work had been attempted before, although English price history has been an energetically worked topic for over a century. Scottish prices in contrast were less commonly encountered in the available sources, and when they could be found tended to be isolated cases rather than the long runs of comparable prices so fruitfully exploited by the likes of Thorold Rogers, William Beveridge, and David Farmer south of the border. We have, however, collected almost six thousand Scottish prices up to 1542 for a range of some 24 different commodities, but these prices still do not provide anything like an even coverage either chronologically or geographically.

The difficulty of trying to compare prices from different regions was merely one of a number of problems. Not only did prices vary from place to place, but so too did the very units of measurement by which commodities were sold. Moreover, the complications of weights and measures were compounded by the difficulties arising from a complex and changing Scottish currency. Nevertheless, despite these very real problems, it has been our experience that collecting the evidence for prices, weights and measures and the coinage has been the first step towards understanding them.

The study of prices has also had some rather less narrowly economic by-products. In order to understand the price data it was obviously necessary to explore something of the background to the production of the various commodities studied. For example, most obviously, the seasonal pattern of the harvest year had a marked influence on the behaviour of cereal prices within any year. Similarly, salt manufacturing processes needed to be explored if its price was to be understood. Equally, consumption habits had an enormous bearing on prices. As a result of considerations of this sort, the whole subject of price history becomes far less narrow than it is sometimes perceived to be.

A brief look at bread prices may illustrate some of these themes. Aberdeen had preserved by far and away the most extensive fifteenth-century sources of any Scottish burgh.[2] And the medieval burgh regarded the regulation of bread prices as one of its most obvious functions. The assize (or fixing) of bread survives from fourteenth-century documents which speak of this sort of price regulation as introduced nationally by David I. However, medieval lawyers had a tendency to ascribe any legislation of uncertain antiquity to David, and it may be that the custom of setting the price of bread in accordance with the cost of wheat did not become established till later in the twelfth or thirteenth century. However that may be, the fourteenth-century documents reveal a system of some sophistication in full working order. The central point to grasp is that it was the weight of the loaf which varied with the price of grain, while the price remained fixed at a halfpenny or a penny. By the fifteenth century twopenny loaves become common because halfpenny loaves would by then have been inconveniently small, but the principle of a more or less fixed price loaf and a widely fluctuating weight held true. For one thing, alterations in the weight of the loaf permitted a much greater degree of flexibility in pricing than if prices had had to rise or fall in convenient money-denominations.

Marked harvest fluctuations were common, and wheat prices could double from one year to the next. Moreover, even similar harvests in successive years would permit a fair degree of variation in price as the post-harvest glut succeeded spring-time scarcity. Burgh regulation of bread prices could do little to protect the town from fluctuation in the price of wheat[3] which was a law of nature, but it was intended to prevent the bakers from exploiting price fluctuations for their own advantage. Thus the aasize of bread calculated the appropriate weight of bread which the bakers ought to supply for any given price of wheat. In addition to the annual variation in wheat prices arising from harvest fluctuations, a long-term rise in wheat prices is apparent from the thirteenth century onwards.[4] This long-term trend explains the shift from halfpenny to penny and twopenny loaves already mentioned, but it also caused the established relationships of bread weight to wheat price to come under especial strain when the rising cost of wheat moved off the end of the sliding scale as envisaged fifty or one hundred years earlier.[5]

Controlling the price of bread inevitably also involved supervising its quality. The two are inextricably linked because price control was based on an assessment of how many loaves might be baked from a given quantity of wheat, and that calculation hinged not only on the weight of the loaf but also on the amount of flour derived from the wheat. Thus, while wholemeal flour utilised all the wheat (less unavoidable wastage and milling costs), finer flours sieved out the bran. In fact even the well-bolted (sieved) bread of the middle ages would have seemed coarse to use, because of the finer silk bolting cloths introduced in more recent times. Nevertheless the medieval customer recognised a range of breads of different qualities.

This range of breads is most clearly displayed in the English sources. Southampton medieval regulations name nine different varieties.[6] The Scottish evidence describes a somewhat simpler situation with fewer named varieties coming down to us, but the Cromertie MS version of the fourteenth-century Scottish assize does give a fair amount of detail about the types of bread available in medieval Scotland. The first loaf described by the assize was the half-penny wastel. This was a white, well-bolted bread, though it is fair to assume that by twentieth-century standards it may have appeared rather grey and course, and distinctly solid. The quachet loaf, on the other hand, was more deliberately fermented or risen, and must have given a less dense loaf.[7] Symnel bread was a better-bolted loaf than the wastel and was therefore dearer, in the sense that the assize prescribed lighter symnel than wastel loaves for any given wheat price. Mixed corn bread, only bolted once, and wholewheat bread, should have weighed half as much again as the quachet. The cheapest bread, panis de trayt and de omni blado, weighed twice the weight of the quachet.

The Aberdeen evidence supplies a few more terms in use in fifteenth-century Scotland. Fowat and craknel were two separately priced varieties superior to unspecified bread.[8] One penny bought 20 oz of bread in the spring of 1486, but only 16 oz of fowat, and 12 oz of craknel. Two years earlier, in a much harder year, the price difference had been less marked, the penny buying 12 oz of bread but only 10 oz of fowat or craknel. We do not know exactly what these varieties may have been, though craknel may have implied a fat-enriched or fried or crisped type of bread, while fowat may have been some kind of cake baked in the ashes.[9] We also meet rye bread in Aberdeen quite commonly. It is almost always cheaper than the corresponding wheat loaf, and comes in similar varieties, bolted and unbolted. Twice some well-bolted rye bread was additionally described as 'sourit' or specially risen.[10] The rye seems to have been usually imported from the Baltic, but wheat was also commonly imported, often from England, and there were regulations against mixing flour of different origins in a single dough. More usually, the quality of the loaf was jeopardised by the addition of 'greit', 'outtakings', 'clecc' or 'brunn', all of which may have been removed form the better-bolted flours but illicitly added to the unbolted.

Cake in the Aberdeen sources refers always to oatcakes, a cheaper food than bread, which of course was the sense in which Marie-Antoinette so famously used the term. It is sometimes observed that although the assize of bread testifies to considerable concern on the part of the authorities to regulate the price of bread, there seems to have been no such concern to monitor the costs of the food of the poorest members of burgh society. In fact very occasionally cake prices were regulated,[11] but the general point that bread prices were controlled and oatcake prices were not does usually hold. The explanation, however, does not lie in a callous disregard for the interests of the poor. Though such an attitude may have been prevalent, the assize of bread was concerned to monitor the profits of the craft, while cake-baking was almost always reserved to the private household. It was forbidden to bake cakes for resale. The interests of the poor were served instead by regulation of the market in grain, which attempted to ensure a fair price undistorted by monopoly. Forestallers and regraters were hounded by authorities who knew they were powerless to protect the people from bad harvests but were determined to prevent any man taking profit from another's necessity.

The assize of bread in Scotland thus raises a number of important questions which can hardly be answered here, although it may be appropriate to note some of them as some kind of agenda for future work. It is not known what proportion of the population of fifteenth and sixteenth-century Aberdeen usually ate bakers' bread rather than baking their own[12] or depending on oatmeal. Oatmeal has a higher calorific value than wheatflour,[13] but it is safe to assume that most people would have preferred wheaten bread if they could have afforded it, and we know also that the living standards of Europe's poorest people were probably higher in the fifteenth and early sixteenth centuries than earlier or immediately afterwards. Much work has been done on the relative importance of bread and meat in historical diets, but it would be equally interesting to explore the boundaries between bread and oatmeal consumption. Unfortunately, the medieval sources may not permit us to make much progress. The question would also touch on the differences between life in town and country. It would also raise again some of the familiar debates about Aberdeen's merchant elite and its apparently long-suffering, much regulated craftsmen, though happily this particular argument has recently been considerably informed by studies from other Scottish burghs.

Notes and References

1. This project was funded for one year by the University of Oxford, and for a further two years by the ESRC. This support permitted the appointment of Dr Elizabeth Gemmill as research assistant, and our joint publication *Medieval Scottish Prices* is currently approaching completion.
2. Dr Gemmill and I are especially grateful to Judith Cripps for her help with our work on the Aberdeen sources, and we join with all historians of Scotland in the gratitude they must feel to the city fathers who guarded these records through the ages.
3. Though the burgh did from time to time import cereals on a corporate basis in an attempt to guarantee supply and an equitable distribution at a just price.
4. The causes of this long-term trend are a matter of much debate, and different factors may have predominated at different times, but among the variables to be considered we may list population change, monetary disturbance, and climatic change.
5. Without pursuing the point too far now, it is enough to note that the bread-weight/wheat-price relationship describes a curved rather than a flat line graph, so merely extending the graph to allow for wheat prices higher than those originally envisaged, significantly altered the bakers' profit margins. Indeed in Paris the whole bread-weight/wheat-price system actually collapsed in 1439 after the notorious harvests of that time sent wheat prices soaring. Thereafter Paris fixed its bread weights permanently, allowing prices to move. See F. Braudel, *The Structures of Everyday Life* (1985), 139, who notes, however, that changing the weight of the loaf remained the norm elsewhere from Venice to Cracow.
6. See most conveniently A. S. C. Ross, 'The Assize of Bread' *EcHR* 2, 9, 1956, 332–42. Braudel, *op. cit.*, 139, mentions a much more limited number of varieties met in the French sources, viz: chailli, bourgeois and brode bread.
7. In England this was known as cocket bread, panis levatus, though the other loaves were probably not entirely unleavened. The Scots rules required the quachet to weigh slightly more than the wastel, apparently to compensate for the way the risen loaf seemed to stretch any given weight of flour.
8. Aberdeen Council Records, volume VI, 238, 832. Assize of bread, 8 March 1484, 2 March 1486.
9. M. Robinson, ed., *The Concise Scots Dictionary*, Aberdeen 1985.
10. Aberdeen Council Records VIII, 866, 4 Sept. 1508; XII i, 260, 21 Oct. 1527. Sour dough remains a reliable method of raising a loaf.
11. Aberdeen Council Records VI, 883, Assize of cake 8 oct 1484.
12. The freemen of Aberdeen were all entitled to have a bread oven, but bread could be baked for private use in a pot. Commercial bread ovens have been excavated, and that found in Aberdeen may be the very one mentioned in the town's earliest surviving court roll. The later ovens in Edinburgh castle, which can still be seen, give some idea of what was involved. However, Braudel calculates that even in early seventeenth-century Venice almost 50% of the city's bread was home-baked.
13. *McCance and Widdowson's The Composition of Foods*, Fourth Edition of MRC Special Report no 297, by A. A. Paul and D. A.

T. Southgate, HMSO 1978, 39, 43 and 51. Oatmeal yields 401 kcal per 100g, wholemeal wheat flour only 318 kcal. Oatcakes have 441 kcal per 100g, while wholemeal bread has only 216 kcal. Since oats were also cheaper than wheat, there can be little doubt about the most economical way to fill the belly.

The Garrabost Meal Mill, Lewis [Map Ref NB 507 325]

The following notes were compiled by the miller, John Morrison, in April 1988.

Shortly after the Meal Mill at Willowglen in Stornoway was burned down, Lady Matheson granted a charter in 1893 for ground at Allt-nan-Gall in Garrabost upon which to build a Meal Mill. Allt-nan-Gall would supply water for driving the mill wheel (*roth mór a'mhuilinn*). A sluice-gate was fitted to Loch Drollabhat near Swordale and two earth dams were constructed, one near the Mill and one about 100 yards further up the burn from the main road.

The Mill was built at Garrabost for the benefit of crofters in the Point area. A Mill operated at Gress to service the villages on the other side of Broad Bay for some time after the opening of the Garrabost Mill.

All the crofts in the various villages of Point, and indeed all over the Island, were fully cultivated, producing quantities of oats, barley, potatoes, turnips etc. By far the commonest cereal crop at the turn of the century and until the second world war was barley or bere.

Shortly after the commencement of the first world war my late father, Angus Graham Morrison of Habost, Ness, came to Garrabost from Vancouver to take over the running of the Mill. At that time the Mill was very busy, working day and night in season producing barley meal and oat meal. The kiln fire was kept burning from Monday morning until Saturday evening during the months of October to February, when many crofters brought their own grain. The writer can well remember some crofters kiln-drying and milling as many as ten or twelve sacks of grain each winter during the 1920s.

Ten hundredweight bags of barley would produce as much as six bolls of barley meal, one boll being ten stones. The amount of meal produced from the same weight of oats is considerably less. The crop was threshed either by *suathadh*, rubbing the grain with the feet, or by using the *sùist*, flail, or later with the aid of small hand-powered threshing mills. The grain was winnowed on a day when there was a good breeze of wind, which carried away any loose chaff or foreign material. Having cleaned, prepared, and bagged the barley or oats, the sacks were then marked by sewing onto each sack a piece of coloured wool or cloth. It was then taken to the kiln at the Mill where it was dried using good dry peats. This process took 4–5 hours, the grain being turned over at internals to prevent burning. In some villages there was a small kiln and the writer can remember one at Aird and one at Portvoller. The barley or

The meal riddle or sifter at Garrabost Mill. Photo: Rachel Freeman.

oats was dried until all the moisture had been removed and the grain was so hard that it could be cracked between the teeth. It was then re-bagged, and the sacks carried on the back into the Mill.

The first process involved emptying the grain into the hopper, *an drabhailt*, of the shelling stones, *muilinn sgilidh*. As the grain fell into the eye of the stones, *sùil a' mhuilinn*, and passed between the rotating upper stone and the stationary nether stone, the husk was cracked. Thereafter it fell down a chute into the shelling sifter or rattler, *criathair*, which separated the dust, *dùdan*. This dust was in great demand for feeding to cattle along with boiled potatoes.

The grain fell over the end of the sifter into a strong breeze of wind, produced by fast-rotating fanners, which carried away the husks, *sgealbach*. *Sgealbach* was sometimes boiled for animal feed with potatoes or turnips but has little nutritional value.

Having finished the shelling process, *sgileadh*, the grain was transferred by an elevator to the hopper of the milling stones. The upper millstone weighs about one and three-quarter tons, and as the grain passed between it and the nether millstone it was ground to very fine meal. The small amount of fine husk left adhering to the grain after the shelling operation fell down the chute along with the meal on to the meal sifter. This sifter, *criathair na mìne*, moved rapidly with a circular motion and separated the *sids* or *cà* from the meal. The meal passed through two sifters incorporated in the one frame. The end result was that the meal was pure, clean and free from any *sids* which fell into a separate bag. *Sids* were always taken home along with the meal as it was considered to be good animal feeding.

The writer well remembers how satisfied and thankful many of the crofters were as they went home from the Mill with three, four or even six bolls of meal. Quite often one boll or more was exchanged at the Mill for a similar quantity of flour meal.

During the years of the first world war and the early twenties there was much meal produced at the Garrabost Mill, the record being in 1917 when 1,700 bolls (106 tons) of meal was produced for the people of Point alone.

Because there were times of water scarcity, an oil engine was purchased in 1909 and fitted to the Mill. This is a fairly large single piston engine burning paraffin fired by hot tube ignition. The piston diameter is 11 inches and the stroke about 22 inches. It has two large fly wheels (each about five and a half foot diameter) giving it considerable momentum. This engine has been restored to working order.

After the second world war crofts in rural Lewis ceased to be cultivated because of the changing economy, and so the Mill at Garrabost, in common with many up and down the country, was no longer needed and ceased to function. It was very useful in its time and a tremendous improvement on the old horizontal water mills which had been common in Lewis, and especially on the quern, *bràth*, which had been used for hundreds of years. The Garrabost Mill was fully automated. No handling was necessary from the time the grain went into the shelling hopper, *an drabhailt sgilidh*, until it was bagged as meal from the meal sifter, *an criathair mòr*.

Ethnological Noticeboard

The Ninth Ethnological Food Research Congress

The Ninth Ethnological Food Research Conference was held in Ireland on 17–22 June 1992, under the organisation of Dr Patricia Lysaght of the Department of Irish Folklore, University College, Dublin.

The theme was Milk and Milk Products, a topic very much in line with a major aspect of the economy of Ireland. The Conference was attended by representatives of 17 countries. It was a particular pleasure to welcome Dr Linda Dumpe from Riga in Latvia, attending the Food Research Congress for the first time as a sign of the opening-out of scholarly activities in European ethnology. On the other hand it was disappointing that a number of regular attenders from Central Europe were unable to attend, as a result of financial constraints.

The Conference was unusual in being peripatetic. It started in Dublin, where Professor John Kelly, Registrar of UCD, and Professor Bo Almqvist, Director of the Department of Irish Folklore, gave addresses of welcome and the two opening lectures were delivered, the first by the Congress President, Anders Salomonsson from Lund in Sweden, and the second by Dr Eszter Kisbán, from Budapest in Hungary. It then moved to Kilfinane Education Centre in Co. Limerick, where a further series of important papers on aspects of milk and milk products in various countries was presented. It also made a splendid centre for field visits to the Golden Vale, the great dairying area in the Republic of Ireland, to see dairying activities at the level of small-scale farming as well as of a highly advanced commercial creamery.

From there the congress moved to Lisdoonvarna in Co. Clare, with visits to Bunratty Folk Park and to the fine scenery of the Burren.

As always, the Congress provided an excellent occasion for meeting colleagues from other countries and for discussion of topics of all kinds - not only dairy products. Exchanges of ideas are always amongst the main benefits of such meetings, but for the specific topic, the papers are currently being edited by Dr Patricia Lysaght and will make a most valuable contribution to ethnological literature. They will be published by Canongate Academic.

MA in Welsh Ethnological Studies

We offer a warm welcome to the setting up of an MA in Welsh Ethnological Studies. This programme is offered jointly by the staff of the Welsh Folk Museum of the National Museum of Wales and the staff of the Department of Welsh, University of Wales, Cardiff. The combined expertise of the staff of both institutions enables an interesting and varied programme of study. The extensive resources of the Museum and the University provide quite exceptional study facilities for the student.

The Welsh Folk Museum is one of the major folk museums of Europe. It possesses a superb collection of buildings, artefacts, implements, and furniture exemplifying the

Welsh vernacular tradition. In addition, it has a substantial tape archive which provides a rich vein of oral documentation and evidence of social customs, folk dance and music, folktales, and the dialects of the Welsh language. The Museum's resources have attracted students of folklore and folk-life from all over the world.

The Department of Welsh, University of Cardiff is one of the most prominent in Wales. It was founded over a century ago and has a fine scholastic record. Staff research interest and expertise lie in the field of Medieval Welsh narrative, Welsh medieval love poetry, dialect studies and the sociolinguistics of Welsh.

The programme of the course combines both coursework and a thesis. In addition to a basic introductory and research methods course, candidates take two of the following options:

Welsh Community Life
Welsh Traditional Music and Customs
Homes and Home Life in Wales
Welsh Folk Narrative: Medieval and Modern
Language and Society in Wales
The Literature of Modern Wales.

(All the options may not be available in a given year. Candidates should always check availability with the Department.)

The course is for full-time students only, with an existing university degree or an equivalent professional qualification. It runs for one academic year, and requires written course work and a thesis. Anyone interested should write for further details and application forms to: The Registrar, University of Wales, College of Cardiff, PO Box 78, Cardiff CF1 1XL.

Pictish Arts Society

The Pictish Arts Society was formed in the mid-1980s to affirm the importance of the Pictish culture to Scotland's historic and prehistoric past. It is actively interested in all aspects of the early history of Scotland and in the development of research and field work. It publishes an informative Journal three times a year, and runs a programme of field trips. On these, several hitherto unidentified Pictish and other historic stones have been discovered.

To cater for membership outside Edinburgh, a conference has been run at Letham, near Forfar, and others are planned elsewhere. A rapidly growing archive is housed in the National Monuments Record of Scotland in the premises of the Royal Commission on the Ancient and Historical Monuments of Scotland, where the Society Archivist has storage and working space. A programme of publication of Occasional Papers has been commenced. The NMRS has sought the assistance of its membership in updating 'Pictish Symbol Stones, a Handlist'.

Membership is open to individuals, groups, and corporate bodies on a local or international basis who wish to support the Society's work.

For a brochure and the current winter programme write to the membership Secretary, Pictish Arts Society, 27 George Square, Edinburgh, EH8 9LD.

T. E. Gray, Secretary

Reviews

FLITTING THE FLAKES.
The dary of J. Badenach, a Stonehaven farmer (1789–1798).
Ed. Mowbray Pearson
Aberdeen University Press and National Museums of Scotland (1992)
viii & 325pp £25. ISBN 1 85752 008 4

To the ordinary reader, especially to one unversed in country matters, the title will probably mean nothing and in its English translation, 'moving the hurdles', convey little more. So it was wise of the editor to add the sub-title, which describes succinctly the book's subject and content.

James Badenach was a small landowner in Kincardineshire and to boot a graduate in medicine of, apparently, Edinburgh, and his chief interest was in agriculture and all its works. To his own farm of Whiteriggs near Fordoun he added a few more which he let out, keeping the Mains and Whiteriggs under his own management. Every day, Sundays excepted, for eight years he noted in precise terms the weather in which he took a particular interest, the work done, the state of the crops, the special activities at seedtime and harvest, visits to neighbours to compare notes on the growth of corn and to market to record the prices. This is the regular pattern of the entries for some 240 pages and it must be admitted that only the brass-bowelled specialist in agriculture or climatology is likely to get through to the end at the first sitting.

The diarist sounds a pretty dry pernickety 'mannie' and one is not surprised to read that his employees once mutinied. Badenach calls it a 'sedition', the current bogey work of the British Government, and it is curious that it all happened just a week after the news of the French king's execution from which we just glimpse where the good doctor's sympathies lay. But though he seldom strays from the single-mindedness of his record, he was sharp-eyed too and observant of incidentals and steps occasionally into slightly more frivolous matters, the bursting of the spring flowers, the larks singing for the first time, even the appearance of toads after their hibernation, and one season when there were few swallows and no butterflies. There are sidelights too into such things as holidays, one day a year at Christmas Old Style (5 January) with a few fast days enjoined by the Kirk and, in 1795, one extra concession of a half day to attend the wedding of one of the men on the farm, though all had to rise earlier that morning to make up for it. And in an odd year they had a harvest feast.

Apparently as a diversion Dr Badenach took to salmon net fishing on the Bervie Water in 1795, but the catch was so poor that he lost interest and does not refer again to this activity. Further afield he reports the wreck of a large ship from Aberdeen at Cove Bay some twenty miles away. Again as a land owner he was involved in the statutory provision of labour in the making of the new turnpike road and attended a meeting to make arrangements but with much scepticism that anything would come of it. Later he set some of his men to cart shingle for road metal.

But the most interesting allusions are to the war with revolutionary France which broke out in February 1795 and to its consequences for the farm. A troop of cavalry stations at Montrose provided a steady market for the hay crop, prices rose in general, especially for fat cattle, but were offset by a steady rise in wages over a decade, which obviously gave Badenach great concern (as it still does with the National Farmers' Union). The price of grain fluctuated a good deal and due to bad harvests corn was at times so scarce as to cause meal riots against its export in various towns.

Of the war itself there is little said. Stonehaven

was well away from its epicentre but Aberdeen is reported as swarming with soldiers in the summer of 1795, and Badenach's second son joined the navy as a cadet at the same time, his father conveying him to Aberdeen and taking the chance to survey the state of farming en route. In February 1797 he mentions the general fear of a French invasion and in October there is the laconic entry, 'Destruction of Dutch fleet', a reference to Admiral Duncan's victory at Camperdown which saved the situation.

The real value of the diary, however, is in its agricultural content, the meticulous recording of the weather (which during the period was preponderantly wet and stormy and which first drew the attention of an editor with similar interests in climate), the daily detail of the multifarious jobs on the farm—ploughing, sowing, reaping, draining and ditching, etc—and as a pleasant and rather unusual bonus for the general reader, a journal of the garden which produced its full quota of vegetables and fruit and caterpillars and was especially rich in early flowering shrubs and plants and bulbs in a variety which would put many a modern farm garden to shame.

There is not much new in this diary of the late eighteenth century. The agricultural revolution had been gathering momentum for decades and its features had already been delineated in the classic accounts of Dickson, Maxwell, Macintosh, Wight and others and the contemporary series of *General Views* of counties drawn up by the Board of Agriculture. The era of the turnip and the potato and crop rotation had long been ushered in and farming was already settled into the routine which, basic mechanisation apart, it was to follow till the Second World War. But Badenach's diary fills in the daily details with impressive fullness.

The editor in his introduction has simplified the reader's task by rearranging the matter thematically under headings like weather, practice, livestock, servants, markets, prices, transport, and there is an appendix of farm rentals, and the amounts of meal apportioned as part payment of wages. A glossary of Scots words is also annexed and raises one or two queries about the reading of the text: there is no such thing as 'birled' barley (p.64)—read 'boiled' barley, fed to horses; and the 'Earth Worm called Tom vulgo' which 'hath spoilt much oats' (p.190) is also a misnomer for 'torie'. Nor does 'hodges' (p.220) look right either unless it might be thought to be a spelling variant of 'hutch'.

So we get from the diary a remarkably clear insight into farm management at the end of that truly innovative eighteenth century, always bearing in mind that we are dealing with the mains of a laird of some substance and professional status. The diaries of some of his smaller tenants might read rather differently. This one is in fact the first of a series of such diaries and accounts planned by the European Ethnological Research Centre and in its handsome format is an impressive introduction to more of its kind. For the agricultural historian especially it will repay the closest study and even the cursory reader will be left with a feeling of respect for a peasantry who endured with dogged patience and perseverance the worst the elements could throw at them to make two blades of grass and two stalks of corn grow where only one grew before.

And it is worth remembering by way of comparison that the countryside described in such sober matter-of-fact terms by Badenach was the same one about which Lewis Grassic Gibbon wrote the most moving elegy in *Sunset Song*.

DAVID MURISON

THE BUSINESS DIARIES OF SIR ALEXANDER GRANT

Ed. James S. Adam

John Donald Publishers Ltd., Edinburgh (1992)

134 pp. Illus. £12.50. ISBN 0 85976 349 8

There is much international interest at the present time in the diaries of farmers, craftsmen and tradesmen. These are turning up in surprising numbers in several countries of Europe. They are being studied and analysed for the detail they provide about individuals who lived and worked in closely defined localities. The present work is the diary of a man who worked in a national and then international field, so it is different in kind. Nevertheless it is a portrayal of the working life of an individual, the son of a Forres railway guard, born in 1864, who rose from being an apprentice baker to being the head of McVitie & Price, the firm which was the parent of the international group, United Biscuits plc.

The diaries cover the years 1917–1937 and include some of the major highlights of Alexander Grant's life. He was granted the Freedom of the City of Edinburgh in 1923, and of London in 1930. He received his Baronetcy on 3 June, 1924. He translated his prosperity, built on the basis of professional skills and management expertise, into acts of generosity, of which the most notable was the benefaction of 1923 that allowed the establishment of The National Library of Scotland. He also supported the purchase of the Monymusk Reliquary, thus ensuring for the nation one of the most precious treasures to be held now in the National Museums of Scotland.

These are examples of the things for which he will be publicly remembered. They are almost laconically entered in the Diaries. Much more space is given, however, to his day-to-day activities, about which selections have been made by the Editor. On the one hand there appears a picture of an individual: a strict disciplinarian with a kindly sense of fellow-feeling that led him to give support to employees in genuine trouble; a thrifty man who took care of pennies but was not afraid to spend in updating equipment—in replacing horse-drawn vehicles with Albion vans and Leylands, in widening the international ramifications of his company from Edinburgh, Manchester and London to other countries of Europe also. Steady growth was a hallmark of the company. The Diaries show it during the war years, coping with shortages of sugar and fats, yet never ceasing to innovate, whether at the level of an office type-writer or book-keeping machine, or of chain ovens in the works, or of new biscuit types, all of which Alexander Grant seems to have personally tested in a constant endeavour to maintain quality. The end of post-war restrictions opened the doors to increased international trade. Butter, for example, was got from Ireland, Siberia, the Argentine and Denmark as well as from home. In biscuit making Continental tastes were taken into account. The sweet-toothed English used a sweet chocolate for a sweet biscuit, whilst on the Continent they preferred an unsweetened chocolate with it and 'were using 60% of beans and 40% of sugar for their sweet biscuits. I think we should try something of the same' (p. 70).

Behind all this detail lies the broader picture of the historical growth of industry during and after the First World War, with its questions of labour management and interaction with unions, and of distribution and sales not only through numbers of travellers going about the country, but also through advertising campaigns. By 1929, Grant was prepared to spend upwards of £20,000 a year on advertising using a professional agency, to help to compete with trade rivals by keeping in the forefront of the public mind the brand-name delicacies, the Jaffas, the Butterette biscuits, Cream Crackers, Venetian Wafers, Cafe Noir, Bunty Creams, Garibaldi and much else. The Diaries give insight into important aspects of the history of the baking side of the food industry and show the beginnings of the every-growing intensity of interaction between food, advertising and the public.

ALEXANDER FENTON

FROM ABERDEEN TO OTTAWA IN EIGHTEEN FORTY-FIVE

The Diary of Alexander Muir

Ed. G. A. Mackenzie

Centre for Scottish Studies, Aberdeen (1990)

131pp, illus.

This book takes the form of a letter-diary. It is an account of a visit to Canada in 1845 by an Aberdeen lawyer, Alexander Muir. He travelled aboard the barque, *Lord Seaton*, a colonial-built vessel of a kind then invading the British shipbuilding market. He gives an impressive account of the expanding settlement around Quebec, Ontario and Montreal, reflecting also the excitement of the exploitation of seemingly endless natural resources, especially in timber, the opening up of clearings to farming, and the beginnings of steam navigation. A canoe trip up the Ottawa river brought him into contact with rough living conditions (sleeping wet, wrapped in a plaid) and a certain amount of danger, but such backwoods conditions contrasted also with the growing sophistication of the towns such as Montreal where, in Rasco's Hotel, he was faced with a French-style bill of fare that included soup and macaroni, fish, lamb, veal, game, poultry, beef, mutton, a choice of at least seven sweets, and wines and liqueurs in abundance.

Muir was visiting relatives. He made his own ripples, being invited by the Chairman of the Dalhousie District Agricultural Society to see a ploughing match with 15 ploughs at Bytown (Ottawa), and being appointed one of the judges of livestock at a local Show. Many such activities closely parallel what would have been happening in the farming districts at home. The closeness of the links between the areas he visited and North East Scotland is striking, and is further emphasised by the detailed information on sources of origin of families provided in the editor's extensive and meticulous notes.

Attitudes of the times come through on occasion—casual shooting at dolphins ('puffy dunders') from the decks of the *Lord Seaton*, or at ducks from a canoe, for fun; the evident dislike of 'Yankees' noted in the Ottawa area; the response to viewing high mass in the Roman Catholic Cathedral in Montreal as 'a most unmeaning thing'; and there is an occasional reflection of dialect speech, for example 'I remembered upon them' (I min't on..).

This letter diary is a well-observed first-hand account of emigrant conditions aboard ship—by no means unpleasant in Muir's case—of a country being opened up to industry, agriculture and commerce, and of family links between the new and the old countries. Added to this are the extensive annotations, which make the publication a useful source book of information on genealogy, on boats, boat ownership, and much else.

ALEXANDER FENTON

THE REV DR ARCHIBALD CLERK'S 'NOTES OF EVERY THING'.

Kilmallie Parish Minister's Diary of *c.* 1864

Ed. Janet Gallon

Kilmallie Parish Church (1987)

74pp, Index, Illus.

This manuscript commonplace book, kept irregularly between 1858 and 1864 and preserved in the collections of the West Highland Museum, Fort William, is published in its entirety and augmented with an account of the author and of his family. The biographical account of its author, Rev. Dr. Archibald Clerk, is a contribution to Scottish historical studies as well as to Celtic studies. Dr. Clerk (1813–1887), a serving parish minister of the Church of Scotland, also occupied an important place in the mainstream of Gaelic scholarship in the nineteenth century, carrying out a revision of the Gaelic bible in collaboration with Rev. Dr. Thomas MacLauchlan.

Clerk was the son of a farming family in Lorne. His father had read Classics at Glasgow University and then returned to the family farm in Glen Lonan and 'reared black cattle and read Latin in Lorne till he was upwards of ninety years of age'. Dr Clerk served in three parishes before embarking on a long ministry of forty-three years in the large West Highland parish of Kilmallie between 1844 and his death in 1887. It has been the largest parish in Scotland with almost 450 square miles of some of the roughest terrain in the Highlands. More than 85% of the parish's population were Gaelic speakers according to the 1881 Census.

Most of the material belongs to one year, 1864. The Minister appears to make a random summary of leading international events of 1863 including deaths of kings and statesmen, the American Civil War, wars or the threat of war in Mexico, Schleswig-Holstein, China, Japan and New Zealand. Besides these, local affairs merit a mention such as local weather, comments on abundance and scarcity of crops, market prices of animals. He concludes laconically, for example: 'Sheep very high in price...Horses dirt cheap'. The arrangement of the Notes in their published form places at the end material recorded in 1858 and 1862 before the original manuscript book had been reversed and re-started. In some respects, the earlier material sets the tone of the book with local history anecdotes, proverbial material and weather lore (especially what he calls 'Faoilteach Rhymes'), and should perhaps have been used as the introductory rather than concluding section to maintain the chronology of the work, which may be seen primarily as an *aide memoire* for the author.

Dr. Clerk seems to have been thinking about beginning a folklore collection and joining the field of Celtic Studies as one or two other ministers were then doing. It may be no more than coincidence that the main bulk of the material begins shortly after the publication of the first edition of J. F. Campbell of Islay's *Popular Tales of the West Highlands*. Indeed he only seems to take up the pen when he has heard a good story or historical tradition from his parishioners. Musings on Lochaber Banquo legends or the origins of the MacGillonie Camerons are good examples.

Noteworthy are Dr. Clerk's philosophical reflections, especially on the moral character and conduct of his parishioners. Some are offhand comments without further explanation, such as the township of Strontian being 'a hotbed of bigotry', and others are more extended and include moral strictures:

> Most painful fall of Doctor MacIntyre with his own servant girl. I believe him to be a Christian but with a good deal of pride and self-will. I

trust this may lead to humility and charity. He must leave this place.

Others include detail of material culture:

Visited John Cameron, Sluggan. His house is the most wretched I have seen in Lochaber—and is a disgrace to a civilised community—a wretched tumbledown bothy—and a large pig installed by the fireside—the only instance of such Irish custom I have seen. The man is young and strong—by no means very poor. I said all I could to him about his conduct—but I must apply to the landlord. He attends no place of worship.

He noted on 23 May 1864:

My peat cutting was finished only on Friday. I had four spades, for five days, twenty in all—paid £3 16s. for cutting above.

And on 31 May:

Began my turnip sowing today. Got my peats fitted on Saturday.

Religious matters are prominent in the notes. An important feature of almost all such commentary is that it seems to indicate a significant gulf between the Kirk's formal theism and the attitudes and belief of the local people. Their exercise of formal religion beyond the formalities of church attendance draws reiterated criticism reminiscent of the comments of the reformers of the sixteenth and seventeenth centuries. Dr. Clerk's notes may be a late example indicating that religion in pre-literate Gaelic communities was more complex than the Kirk would have wished.

He was alive to the vivid turns of speech of his parishioners and he can employ colourful vocabulary. Captain Cameron or 'Shoulder John'—presumably the translation of an unexplained epithet *Iain Slinnean* or *Iain an t-Slinnein*—was 'married to one of the Meobles [the tacksman family of MacDonald of Meoble]—a wild, half-cracked randy who died several years ago'. He carefully recorded Gaelic words and expressions:

I heard two good words from James MacIntyre—speaking of the character of a neighbour who, while friendly in his way, has no firmness of purpose. Tha e cho neonitheach. Chan eil taic air bith ann. (He is so nothingish. There is no support, substance, in him.)

Examples of lexical rarities are *balgam-ronnach*, *beithir-bheinn*, *casan-fhionain*, *eileach*, *tireil* and *ugad*. The Gaelic content is itself worthy of separate analysis.

Dr. Clerk's commonplace book is an important publication, recording the speech of unlettered folk and monoglot Gaelic speakers, and giving insight into contemporary attitudes and belief. It will repay close study and may even merit a more extensive edition.

HUGH CHEAPE

BÄUERLICHE ANSCHREIBEBÜCHER ALS QUELLEN ZUR WIRTSCHAFTSGESCHICHTE

(Farm Account Books as Sources for Economic History)

K.–J. Lorenzen-Schmidt und B. Poulsen, Eds.

Studien zur Wirtschafts- und Sozialgeschichte Schleswig-Holsteins, Band 21, Neumünster (1992)

244pp.

This volume presents the proceedings of the second major conference of the International Association for Research on Peasant Diaries, which took place in Kiel in 1989.

The two editors begin by establishing the value of farm account books and notebooks as sources for economic and social history. Such sources provide tests of literacy, which now seems to have been more widespread amongst rural populations at early dates than previously thought; they reflect the results of the formal teaching of farming practices at least from the second half of the nineteenth century, though the fact that publishers were producing special booklets to help farm folk from as early as 1788 (in Germany, at least) suggests that their clients were already taking a consciously wider overview of farming beyond the bounds of their own holdings. Of course the advancement of agriculture through improved practices and in conjunction with industrial developments and urban needs has to be looked at as a set of regional phenomena with differing timespans and dates of origin, but a sufficient range of farm diaries and account books, studied in depth, can undoubtedly illuminate relationships between core and periphery farming areas on an all-European basis as well as within national boundaries. Diary and account book sources can also be used as back-up in looking at general historical and economic problems as well as those of a very localised nature.

The following 14 articles look in more depth at matters raised in the introductory article.

Gudrun Gormsen discusses a Danish farm diary of the nineteenth century. Its detail on the work, economy and life of a farmer in a heath area, and on the interrelationships between grazing and arable, on the use of the heath as a major resource, and on manuring has been used as an aid to the reconstruction of economic activities in the Open Air Museum and to the study of their ecological effects.

Esben Hedegaard uses farm note books from West Funen (1793–1874) to look at change over the long term and as between father and son. She also relates the farming data to the macro-history of agricultural improvement in Denmark over a comparable period, asking when agrarian reform began to take a marked effect. The answer is that improvements, other than a generally upward movement marked by better seed–yield rations, seem to relate specifically to the use of marl as a fertilising medium. There are three identifiable phases: 1793–1835, marked by a low level of production, with oat and barley seed–yield ratios of 1:3–4 (much in line with Scottish pre-improvement standards); 1835–40, marked by a jump (perhaps due to marling) of over 100% in crop yields; 1840–63, a period of stability with wheat, rye and barley yields at 1:8–10 and oats 1:6–7. Thus lack of manure, and possibly the set ways of an older father, inhibited participation by this individual farm in the general agrarian improvements in Denmark in their earlier stages.

Jens Holmgaard discusses a Jutland farm diary of 1786–97 and relates it to the agrarian reforms of the late eighteenth century in Denmark. He is concerned to show that there were possibilities for individual development even within the old estate system and that a reappraisal of relationships between manor house and farm would be well worth while.

Karl Peder Pedersen uses the diary of an eighteenth century tenant farmer in Funen to examine problems created by recurrences of the cattle plague. He throws light on the resigned attitude of farmers, who regarded the plague as 'God's will'. Plague led to high cattle prices and dearer dairy products, but had the benefit of giving pasture a rest at a time when agrarian resources, through population growth, were close to their limits. It is clear that plague hindered agrarian reform for an appreciable period, though at the diarist's farm there is evidence of a gradual rise in prosperity even during the plague period, perhaps as a result of diversification into horse-breeding, sheep-rearing and more grain production.

Bjorn Poulsen's contribution is on seven farmers' account books from Schleswig, sixteenth to seventeenth centuries. Trading activities went on alongside farming. It is shown that the writers in question were relatively free and not badly off because the soil quality was good. They were not overly oppressed by their manorial masters, and had the status to be given credit facilities, where needed, for their products. The commercial emphases, at this early period, strike a relatively modern note.

Jonas Berg writes about the Swedish Farm Diary Project run by Nordiska Museet in Stockholm. It has been very successful in identifying sources and incorporating them into a plan of research. One aspect of this is the question of stock-farming and breeding, which he exemplifies from nineteenth-century examples, as an instance of the kind of analysis that becomes possible when diaries have been assembled in sufficient numbers.

Janken Myrdal gives a particularly thoughtful account of his time-distribution studies, also on the basis of the Swedish Farm Diary Project. He sees work-time as a limited resource to be allocated, and not only as a measure for community production. As a method of approach to diary analysis, the counting of days spent on particular tasks can give a rough guide; but a finer grid is achieved by evaluating the number of day-works made, including the number of people involved in each specific job.

Farmers' diaries reflect types of agricultural production. They show the influence of proximity to industry, they demonstrate the symbiosis between farming and pre-industrial types of activity, and they reflect the results of innovations in farming techniques and equipment. Myrdal also shows that the concept of piece-work—as through the use of day-labourers—is pre-industrial, even though it also marks a new concept of time. His work-time diagrams (p. 118) provide an excellent visual means of making comparisons between farm diaries from different times and places.

Jan Peters discusses the Neuholland (former East Germany) Farm Diary Project. From numerous diary and archival sources he and his colleagues have assembled information on the well-doing and prosperous Neuholland dairy farmers. The motivation in their diary writing seems to have been to pass on their experiences to their successors. They were marked by business astuteness in their market strategies. They were also politically astute and had what Peters called 'spiritual mobility' in terms of religion.

Three diaries used, for 1772–1826, 1843–58 and 1859–63, bring a cumulative perspective to the understanding of the economic, social and cultural background, and to the *mentalité* of the farmers of the region.

Manfred Schober's study of a volume entitled 'Oeconomische Adversaria', kept by father and son from 1801–13 and 1831–1875, not only gives detail about a small farming business in Saxony, but also shows how detailed knowledge of an area can extend the possibilities for interpretation. The process is, of course, two-way.

Klaus-J.Lorenzen-Schmidt deals with ten years of research into farm account books in the Elbmarsh area of Holstein, using about 14 sources covering the period 1709–1874. This was a fertile area. Figures for stock numbers and crop yield have been compiled and the source material has been analysed under headings such as agricultural, household, food and workforce needs, local and national taxes, need for manual workers, etc. As in Schleswig, prosperous conditions favoured the giving of credit facilities when required. Lorenzen-Schmidt's work shows how useful a quantitative approach can be in throwing light on the economics of an area.

Helmut Ottenjann, as always, seeks to contextualise his subject, this time in the light of manorial and household inventories, and as part of a continuing probe into the historical study of material culture. He takes into his review account books kept by people other than farmers, such as those of merchants and unions. He notes that though there are difficulties in using such sources, nevertheless they provide much quantifiable data for research, especially when, in any specific region, they are set together in chronological sequence and as far as possible tied together in a geographical net. Such a systematic approach is essential for the firmer development of the subject.

Wiebe Bergsma's contribution of Friesian farmers' diaries relates to what is very much a core area from the viewpoint of European agricultural as a whole. The sixteenth-century Abel Eppens, about whom Bergsma is mainly speaking, is a good example of the kind of man who helped greatly to extend the influence of the farming of the area. He was active in local politics and church affairs, and was a judge, as well as an important farmer.

Hidde Feenstra is also concerned with Friesland using the account books and papers of noblemen from the sixteenth to the eighteenth centuries. He looks at rental changes over time and in different parts of his area, at evaluations of ground owned by nobles, and at questions of peat removal and reclamation.

Maili Blauw examines account books and statistics as sources from economic history, covering much the same area as Bergsma and Feenstra, but concentrating on the nineteenth century. The information provided on cattle, milk cows, young cattle, butter and cheese demonstrates how diary sources can give support to or act as a check on official statistics; and Blauw also makes it clear that diaries and the account books of individuals can add flesh to the bare bones of statistics. Here again, the role of this area as a European farming core is emphasised.

The volume is completed by a 21-page bibliography of diary and account book sources, arranged country by country. It is already a massive basis for future research; and yet there are many countries, such as Hungary and Poland, that are not represented. There are gaps to be filled in this respect also.

ALEXANDER FENTON

THE BUILDINGS OF SCOTLAND

Highlands and Islands

John Gifford

Penguin Books in association with The Buildings of Scotland Trust (1992)
683pp. £30. ISBN 0 14 071071 X

This is the fifth volume in the Penguin *Buildings of Scotland* series, which, managed and financed by the Buildings of Scotland Trust, plans to cover all of Scotland by the end of the century. The volumes that have appeared so far deal with *Lothian, Edinburgh, Fife and Glasgow*. The present volume is the third with which John Gifford has been involved. More is to flow from his pen, but what he has covered already (ranging in the *Highlands and Islands* from the blackhouse at Arnol in Lewis to castles, tower houses and palaces) is already a formidable contribution to the logging of Scotland's architectural heritage.

The objectives of the series, following that of Sir Nikolaus Pevsner's *The Buildings of England*, which was completed between 1951 and 1974, are—as stated by the late Colin McWilliam—'to present all the buildings that merit attention on architectural grounds, to do it for the whole country, and to do it with all possible speed'.

Thorough research is also a hallmark of the series. In effect, the outcome will be one of the most systematic surveys of the buildings of Scotland ever yet achieved.

The work is approached methodically. An Introduction covers the topographic background and the nature of the building material and then works chronologically from prehistoric times to recent days. Not only individual buildings are considered, but also communication systems, and even graveyards. The Highlands and Islands are divided into eleven units so that visitors staying in any one of them can derive maximum benefit. The bulk of the book is taken up with the detailed listing of these areal units and each entry relates to a map at the beginning of each section, so that location is easy. The value of the whole as a handbook is enhanced by a glossary of architectural and related terms, often supported by sketches, and there are copious indexes of artists and of places.

There is a good supporting block of photographs in the middle of the book, ranging from the stones of Stennes in Orkney and the stones of Callanish in Lewis to Dornoch Cathedral, the Trades Loft of St Duthus Memorial Church in Tain, the thatched Laidhay croft buildings (now a museum) in Caithness, and the Spean Bridge Commando War Memorial by Scott Sutherland.

This is not a book to be read in abstract detail. It must be used on the spot, and there thoroughly studied. Those who do so will benefit greatly, with increased knowledge and understanding not only of the buildings, but also of the physical environment in which they stand and the historical and social contexts to which they belong.

ALEXANDER FENTON

THE FARMSTEADS OF THE BATHGATE HILLS

Nils White

West Lothian District Council, Planning Department, County Buildings, Linlithgow (1992)

46pp., 44 photographs, 6 line drawings, map. £1.95
ISBN 0.907.952.038

Compiled after West Lothian Planning Department carried out a survey in 1990, this booklet takes a twentieth-century look at the nineteenth-century farm buildings which pattern the Bathgate Hills in West Lothian, an area fringed by Linlithgow, Torphichen and Uphall.

Fifty steadings in various states of repair were visited, and a detailed report made of each one. It was judged important to record the existence of such buildings and their setting before more twentieth-century change obliterated their valuable 'historical narrative'. Written with the general public's interest in mind, the book helps readers to interpret this historical narrative by showing them where and how to look.

The author, a member of the West Lothian Planning Department, writes concisely and with quiet authority. Building and technical terms are kept to a minimum; the few words indispensable to accurate naming of features are explained at the beginning of the section called 'Construction'.

Thereafter, the book moves from barn to granary, to byre, dairy, stable, bothy and farmhouse, offering brief information in words, drawings and photographs, to give the clearest possible picture of designs and changes, and how these involved the people working and living in the farmsteads. Small detail is not overlooked. A hole in a gable belonged to the resident owl, nineteenth-century vermin exterminator; the small-scale flight of steps helped free-range hens to reach inside nesting places; the doocot in the roof provided fresh pigeon meat.

Finally, the question of the future of the pleasant and still useful buildings is discussed. Most owners are interested in the fate of their properties, and appreciate that successful conversion requires care and a measure of historical perspective.

Professor Fenton, Director of the School of Scottish Studies, in his foreword to the book, confirms that the quality of the buildings is noticeable, and makes a plea for all Local Authorities to recognise that everyday, working buildings are vital constituents in the character of the landscape, and, as such, should be given protection from insensitive change.

The interesting print used for the cover, a photograph dated 1911 of dairy work at Goremire Farm, was supplied by the Scottish Ethnological Archive.

This is a timely, well-balanced publication—guid gear in sma buik.

MARGUERITA BURNETT

THIS NOBLE HARBOUR

A History of the Cromarty Firth

Marinell Ash, eds. James Macaulay and Margaret A. Mackay

Cromarty Firth Port Authority, Invergordon, in association with John Donald Publishers Ltd, Edinburgh

305pp, 72 photographs. Paperback, £9.50. ISBN 0 859763 196

Late in 1984, the Cromarty Firth Port Authority decided to commission a book on the history of their area. This could have been a pedestrian study of local affairs, but the scholar they chose was Dr. Marinell Ash. She set about her task with all her accustomed enthusiasm, and an energetic determination that this should be far more than a narrow catalogue of parochial events.

The Firth is a fascinating subject. Itself one of the finest natural harbours in the world, it has for centuries been a significant point in the network of communications linking Easter Ross with Europe, North America and other parts of the world. Dr. Ash saw its history as both 'a reflection and an exemplar' of what was happening elsewhere in Scotland, and her wide-ranging and authoritative account describes how such major events as the Reformation, agricultural improvements, the Disruption, the Clearances and the coming of the railways and the oilmen influenced an individual community.

Dr. Ash's use of sources is impeccable, combing as it does unpublished manuscript material like kirk session minutes, farm accounts, and legal and exchequer records with parliamentary reports, secondary books and articles, interviews and personal communications. Tales of colourful characters including the murderous Lady Foulis, seventeenth-century ally of witches and 'the little folk', and Sir Hector Munro, the ingenious late eighteenth-century improving landlord, enliven the serious social analysis provided by the text.

Written with humour and verve as well as the professional historian's rigorous respect for the facts, this valuable study is a real contribution to our understanding and enjoyment of Scotland's past. Sad to say, Marinell died before it could be published, but her editors have completed her work in a manner amply befitting her own high standards of scholarship.

ROSALIND K. MARSHALL

TARTAN: THE HIGHLAND HABIT

Hugh Cheape

National Museums of Scotland, Edinburgh (1991)

72pp. £5.95. ISBN 0 948636 23 8.

Despite there being a number of publications on the subject of Scottish Tartans, this slim volume is an interesting and welcome addition. Clearly written by a master of the subject, it is the story of the history of the fabric, how it was used in dress, and of its adoption as the symbolic badge of Scottish kinship.

The evolution of the versatile plaid, the everyday garment of Highland folk in the sixteenth century, is incontrovertibly linked with the development of tartan as we know it today. In ancient times, weavers produced cloth of stripes and checks but it is not until the sixteenth century that the name 'tartan' occurs in records. This was the period of closest Franco-Scottish links and 'tartan' may be a corrupted form of the French word 'tirtaine'. Hugh Cheape leads us through four centuries showing how economic and political events each played their part and how enterprising Scots developed systematised and sophisticated weaving techniques to ensure the survival of tartan. Although George IV had acknowledged a partiality for the fabric, the ultimate stamp of approval was provided by Queen Victoria as a result of her great enthusiasm for the Highlands of Scotland: tartan was here to stay.

The text is accompanied by an excellent selection of photographs: there are over 110, the bulk of them in colour, illustrating all aspects of Highland dress—from the early simple plaids to the expensive products from the fashion houses of Paris. The book is attractively presented, and the author has helpfully provided a further reading list.

DOROTHY SLEE

TO SEE OURSELS—RURAL SCOTLAND IN OLD PHOTOGRAPHS

Harper Collins and the National Museums of Scotland (1992)

160pp, 181 Illus. £15.99. ISBN 0–00–470098–8

Here is a book that will attract a wide audience. It contains a delightful and informative selection of photographs spanning some 80 years from the extensive collections of the Scottish Ethnological Archive of the National Museums of Scotland. It will appeal equally to students of social history and to nostalgics of all ages.

In the introduction Dorothy Kidd explains the intrinsic value of old photographs and indicates the full range of the Archive's activities. The selected photographs have been themed in nine sections: Living with the Land, Harvesting the Sea, At Home, Crafts and Industries, Trade and Transport, Community, Growing Up, Entertainment and As Others See Us. Each section is prefaced with either brief historical notes or personal recollections of the subject, and each photograph is supported by explanatory captions.

The photographs, all in black and white and of people from all parts of rural Scotland, can be likened to a national family album; apart from groups, most of the characters featured are named and are at their workplace, still working or having a short break. We are therefore provided with a rare opportunity of seeing the everyday clothes worn (before they went into the rag rug) and the equipment and methods used on the job. Many of the photographs remind us of the camaraderie engendered by happy groups of workers pulling together in a common purpose, alas now often vanquished by sophisticated machinery.

It is not possible to ignore the fashion trends in the photographs. In the men beards were replaced by moustaches by the 1920s, but it took a little longer for the size of their pancake caps to shrink to more modern proportions and for them to abandon their waistcoats for jerseys or cardigans. The ladies' headgear all but disappears, their hair is cut and their hemlines rise. There were a few pairs of spectacles visible but only three of these were in photographs dated before the 1948 National Health Service Act. I wonder; were their eyes needing attention or was their sight better than today's standards?

Alison Cromarty and Dorothy Kidd have clearly taken great care in selecting the photographs from the many thousands available and in arranging them in such an interesting and effective manner. Greater impact has been achieved by placing related but contrasting situations on adjacent pages: for example, the different images presented by the cottage interiors in 1902 and 1970 on pages 62 and 63; the well-cared-for children having tea and cakes beside the barefooted tousy tinks on pages 122 and 123; and I cannot leave out dear hard-working Lucy Alison, the washerwoman at St Monance in the early 1900s alongside the jolly volunteer dishwashers at Eriskay in 1960 on pages 68 and 69.

This is a powerful collection of photographs permitting us to survey our past with greater intensity than through the written word alone—for example, the dreadful working conditions of the fisher girls on page 51.

This book is the first in a series based on the photographs in the Museum's Archives. It is certain that further productions will be of an equally high quality of interest and information.

DOROTHY SLEE

EXPLORING SCOTTISH HISTORY

A Directory of Resource Centres for Scottish Local and National History in Scotland

Ed. Michael Cox

Scottish Library Association and Scottish Local History Forum, Edinburgh (1992)

161 pp. £6.95. ISBN 0 900 649 79 8

This Directory is the outcome of an excellent initiative in collaboration between the Scottish Local History Forum, the Scottish Library Association, the Scottish Records Association and the Scottish Museums Federation. It provides a ready means of entry to research into the local and national (not always separable) history of Scotland, by listing resource centres, pinpointing their strengths, and providing the names of people who may be contacted. The centres specified may appear diverse at first glance, but there is no single road to history studies, and a rounded understanding of aspects of history such as genealogy, for example, is best gained by trying out a variety of approaches. The Directory also includes information about the collaborating organisation, the National Register of Archives (Scotland), which gives advice to private owners of historical papers, and the question of copyright under the Copyright, Designs and Patents Act 1988.

This is a research tool that should be in everybody's hands.

ALEXANDER FENTON

GUIDE TO THE HISTORY OF TECHNOLOGY IN EUROPE

Janet Carding, Timothy Boon, Nicholas Wyatt and Robert Bud

Science Museum, London (1992)
142 pp. £8.00. ISBN 0 901805 513

This Guide is the first to list those in Europe, covering 26 countries, engaged in the history of technology (800), along with relevant institutions (600) and journals (130). It is an important who's who, what's what and where's where to a subject that in part has well-defined parameters, and that in part is still—especially in terms of the history of technology—examining its relationships with neighbouring disciplines such as industrial archaeology, business history and the history of science. In this capacity, it is an essential research tool for its 10 broad subject areas: generalities, approaches to the history of technology, production technologies, motive power and energy sources, materials and processes, mechanical technologies, civil engineering technologies, transport technologies, electrical and communication technologies, medical and biological technologies. The information presented is based on questionnaires; there are examples at the back of the volume and the intention is that updating should take place from time to time in all the four sections that comprise the volume (lists of researchers, of journals, of institutions, and indices to the whole). The volume well reflects its own subject, for it facilitates contact between scholars and institutions by providing not only names, addresses and phone-numbers, but also fax and E.mail numbers. And if the reader does no more than browse through it, the outcome is inevitably a mass of fresh information and the opening up of new research perspectives.

ALEXANDER FENTON

HISTORY CURATORSHIP

Gaynor Kavanagh

Leicester University Press, (1990)
183 pp., 31 illus., £32.00. ISBN 0-7185-1305-3

The author of this book has been a Lecturer at the Department of Museum Studies,University of Leicester, since 1980. The material is based on 10 years of teaching and of assessment of needs. It is in three parts: the history and present state of history museums; the theories and methods of history curation; and the practicalities of how history museums present their material and interact with the public. The third section is the most museum-orientated; the first two sections, however, consider history museums in a much wider setting, as they have developed through time and as elements to which wider ethnological theories can be applied.

One of the most compelling points is that British museums do not have the unity of approach that is the hallmark of Scandinavian museums (and those of a number of other countries), because there has not been in Britain the kind of university teaching of ethnology that can provide common principles of approach to the subject. It is such background training that has led, especially in Sweden, to a systematically thought-out approach to the documentation of contemporary material culture, especially as it is found in towns and in industry.

Kavanagh emphasises modern society's need for history, and the way in which museums have tried to satisfy this need from Victorian times. At the same time, the ethnological approach (which is reality she is using without calling it that) is beginning to shape interpretation and display so that museums are actually in much closer contact with public needs than they ever were in the past. She outlines the methodology of approach, field-working and recording methods, with full and wide-ranging references to books and articles.

The book is not, however, a handbook. It is a book of ideas, of awareness of objects as part of a complex system of social language. It makes the reader think and is of value not only within museum studies. The title 'history curatorship' is an accurate indication of the book's width of approach. With this, it is a most readable and valuable text book and guide.

ALEXANDER FENTON

VOLKSKUNDE EN MUSEUM: EEN LITERATUURWIJZER

(Ethnology and museum: a guide to the literature)

Jaap Kerkhoven and Paul Post

P. J. Meertens-Instituut voor Dialectologie, Volkskunde en Naamkunde, 19, Amsterdam/ Arnhem (1992)

140pp. ISBN 90 80389 347

Ethnologists and museum people alike will welcome this bibliographical guide. Its parameters are clearly defined. In time, it deals with publications from 1945 onwards, when thinking about the context and role of museums within society gave rise to waves of international activity. Linguistically, it is confined to writings in Dutch, French, German, English and Italian, though these touch on all Western European countries as well as the USA. Emphasis has been laid on periodical literature with an ethnological approach to museum problems, and to this end 51 journals (including *The Review of Scottish Culture*) have been searched for the 980 bibliographic entries. These are presented in four sections: general museum questions; the museum as an organisation (with sub-sections on the formation and management of collections, research and documentation, presentation, education personnel and organisation); individual and open-air museums covering more than one geographical unit, and those confined to a specific geographical unit; and exhibitions.

The compiler (Kerkhoven) and editor (Post), reflecting museum and academic approaches, have worked harmoniously to produce a workmanlike, usable research tool. The Introduction (in Dutch with German summary) gives an analytical overview of the entries. For students being trained in ethnological studies, there is, of course, considerable vocational importance in keeping an eye on the activities of cultural-historical, folk and open-air museums, whether local or larger-scale. This volume has particular importance in this context because European ethnological studies have, on the one hand, greatly influenced such museums, especially since the 1960s, and on the other, changing trends in museum practice reflect changing academic and social viewpoints. For instance, much attention was paid in the past to tracing the origins and geographical spread of practices and objects as part of a quest for national identity or regional character. Now the emphasis is on contextualisation of phenomena within communities, with the involvement of the public in interactive displays and, as part of that, an altogether more commercially orientated approach by museums to changing displays. As part and parcel of all this the everyday life of workers in industry and in towns, including apprentices, has come into focus, along with efforts to present inter-ethnic relationships and ecological problems, and to identify aspects of the urbanisation of the countryside. There has been a levelling of regional forms of material culture, in buildings as well as in smaller tools and equipment, and a transformation of aspects of folklore from its local roots into an unprovenanced 'folklorism'.

The point of this review, however, is not to quote details, but to emphasise how analysis of a specific batch of bibliographical sources has thrown much light on the intellectual developments underlying both ethnological and museum studies over the last several decades.

ALEXANDER FENTON

SONS OF SCOTIA, RAISE YOUR VOICE

Early nineteenth century Scottish broadsides from a collection in Edinburgh University Library

Ed. Peter B. Freshwater

The Friends of Edinburgh University Library. George Square, Edinburgh, EH8 9LJ, 1992

142 pp. 14 illus. £10.00 (£7.50 to members of The Friends of Edinburgh University Library)

The Friends of Edinburgh University Library began to publish the Drummond Book Series in 1976. Named after William Drummond of Hawthornden (1585 – 1649), poet and early benefactor of the Library, the series aims to promote some of the unusual papers and books in the Library's Special Collections. *Sons of Scotia, Raise Your Voice*, which is number four in the Series, draws attention to a motley collection of Scottish broadside ballads pasted into an old minute book, which the late Francis Collinson gave to the Library in 1973.

Peter Freshwater, Deputy Librarian of Edinburgh University Library, and Editor of the book, explains in his introduction that these ballads were chosen because 'they form a representative sample of the Scottish broadside ballad in circulation during the 1830s, especially in Edinburgh' and 'to illustrate the current concerns of everyday life of the period'. The verses are printed with the tunes to which they might have been sung in the streets.

The importance of street music is often overlooked. A great part of the musical life of the population was lived not in the concert hall or salon, but in the streets and tenements, the inns and howffs. Tatty crude broadsides, price a penny (or less), were the poor man's newspapers; they kept him up-to-date with events and 'Mr. Ramsay's new songs'. The marvel is that they survived long enough to become part of a University collection. Walter Geikie's wonderful etchings, four of which are among the illustrations in this book, capture convincingly the street-corner newsagents of the time, the so-called Cadies, and their ragged, eager customers.

What did they read and sing about? From the evidence of the minute book (provenance unknown), its compiler was interested in songs about politicians and politics of the Reform Act of 1832. Ten ballads are political squibs—petty lampoons—of men involved in the passing of this Act. The first line of one of them, 'Reform song', supplies the title of the book. A further twenty ballads purvey current events and traditional sentiment tailored to nineteenth-century taste. Some of the verse is quite dreadful. Rarities include 'Cholera Morbus', a dirge about the 1831/32 epidemic in Edinburgh; 'The Horning Doctor', which rails against a hated tax levied on occupiers but not on owners of property; 'The Election of the Hangman'; and 'The Dandies of Deception', which makes satirical comment on fashionable dress. Among the traditional fare is a version of 'The Laird of Cockpen'; no book of Scottish ballads would be complete without this favourite, celebrated today in seven verses, but here given a further six (authorship unknown) in which Mistress Jean is allowed time to change her mind.

Mr. Freshwater's footnotes at the end of each ballad help the reader to de-code the 1830 insinuations and innuendo woven into the verses, and place them in historical context. He also includes a Who's Who of people referred to in the songs, a note about the printers of broadsides, a select bibliography of sources, and a glossary of Scots words.

The whole adds up to a happy, frequently amusing, amalgam of ballad, music, and social commentary. The Friends of Edinburgh University Library and their Editor have reason to be well satisfied with Drummond Book, Number 4.

MARGUERITA BURNETT

THE CULBIN SANDS—FACT AND FICTION

Sinclair Ross

Centre for Scottish Studies, University of Aberdeen (1992)

196 pp. £7.95 ISBN 0 906265 16 9

The Culbin Sands, now a Site of Special Scientific Interest with a thriving 2560 ha forest which in itself is a field research station of national importance for the study, amongst other things, of all aspects of nutrition deficiency, can in truth also be described as a site of long-standing special human interest. Over the years it has drawn great attention—including that of the present reviewer as a boy on a bicycle, first attracted by the lure of prehistoric artefacts and then captivated by the beauty and solitude of the great stretches of sand-dunes. That the story of the overwhelming of the Kinnairds' estate by blowing sand in the 1690s was largely a fiction originated and maintained by a series of writers, did not cross his mind till much later in life.

Now Sinclair Ross has well and truly set the record straight. Using original source documents located in the Scottish Record Office and elsewhere, and a sequence of 26 sets of maps dating between 1590 and 1974, in alliance with detailed geological, geomorphological and land-use surveys, he has put paid to much mythology of long standing. Nevertheless the story of the shifting sands at the mouth of the Findhorn and of the relationship with the rest of the Moray coast, and their effects over time on patterns of human settlement, is no less exciting than the created fantasies of many previous writers.

Sinclair Ross has gone about his search in a scientific way, piecing together his story from a wide range of sources. He has accumulated and analysed a mass of data and has interpreted it well and readably, showing that, after all, the Barony of Culbin was not the garden and granary of Murray, with sixteen farms thriving and prosperous beyond their neighbours, but a reasonably normal farming (and fishing) estate with six jointly-tenanted farms. The author's instinct for precision is too exact in giving specific averages to terms such as 'plough' (ploughgate) on p. 110 and in his Appendix 12 (p. 183), for there could be variation in extent according to conditions of soil and geography that in turn affected the amount of work the draught animals could achieve. Nevertheless it is possible to sympathise with this serious effort to work out the real arable area used by the Culbin farmers, and the outcome is in any case convincing.

There are some small cavils. It is a pity that the concept of a primitive 'scratch' plough should continue to get into the literature—indeed a team of up to twelve draught animals could hardly fail to do rather more than scratch the surface, and would have to do more to plough it in ridge and furrow fashion. But this and some other small points are minor in relation to the interpretational value of the whole approach, and the mass of fresh information that has been brought to light.

ALEXANDER FENTON

SPALPEENS AND TATTIE HOKERS

History and Folklore of the Irish Migratory Agricultural Worker in Ireland and Britain

Anne O'Dowd

Dublin, Irish Academic Press (1991)

441 pp. £35.00. ISBN 0-7165-2450-3

Spalpeens and Tattie Hokers is a work of sound and wide-ranging scholarship—as befits a good Ph.D thesis—which is also very readable. Clearly and logically laid out, it is based on a thorough sifting of published information, in particular a range of Parliamentary Papers and official documents, and on analysis of data gathered by questionnaires issued by the Department of Irish Folklore of University college, Dublin. The outcome is the first systematic study of the seasonal and temporary migration of Irish workers within Ireland itself, and within England and Scotland.

The internal migration of harvesters, drovers and beggars is well recorded in Ireland from the mid-seventeenth century. Seasonal migration to the rest of Britain followed, until by 1841 a figure of 57, 651 was reached (and this is regarded as a conservative estimate). The flow was maintained until agricultural improvements, new forms of technology, and the use of imported grain from the prairies of America had reduced the need for migrant labour in the 1860s. Balancing this, however, was the fact that the adoption of new crops such as the potato, turnips, hops and fruit, and an increase in market gardens, kept up the demands for seasonal workers. As a result, it was only from the 1880s that a substantial decline in migrants took place, due largely to increased use of machinery and a decline in arable. A temporary upsurge occurred in 1892–1900, then a steady decline which, however, continued far through the twentieth century. But for a time, seasonal migration from certain parts of Ireland was so intensive that Achill Island, for example, could be spoken of as the 'winter home', and migration as a means of earning cash could be not only an essential life-line, but also the sole support of innumerable families.

Migration changed its character through time. At first those taking part were small farmers, cottagers, agricultural labourers, poor folk with families, and occasionally fishers. After the mid-nineteenth century potato famine, women also began to migrate, especially for the Scottish potato harvest.

Movement within Ireland was from poorer to richer areas, especially during the hungry months of June to July. Externally, the Ulster Irish tended to head for Scotland, and those further south went to England via Liverpool. Within each of these countries, patterns of movement were firmly established, and migrant work groups would follow them for year after year, returning to places where work was assured or offering their labour at feeing markets and fairs; piece work was often preferred to daily rates of pay.

The lack of proper accommodation or of sanitary facilities was a constant problem, about which stories are legion. Gradually, following official enquiries into the housing of the working classes—but not until after the First World War—conditions improved as local authorities took a more positive concern and as the Department of Health began to apply regulations.

The Irish were in general not very popular, though for long they filled an essential niche in the farming year. Their host communities were afraid that they might spread disease. The Poor Laws tied the local poor to their own parishes in England and Scotland, but the Irish poor who came had no such restrictions on their mobility and could move freely in search of work or higher wages across parish boundaries. During the two World Wars, the Irish were not subject to conscription and their freedom to travel was further resented. Nevertheless they played an enormous role in the harvest- and potato-fields of Britain for upwards of two centuries, until technology ended the seasonal migrant system.

Anne O'Dowd provides the detail of their lives, and their interactions with the farmers they served. She has also gathered and presented associated folk tales, many of them with internationally recognised motifs, to an extent that amply testifies to the long continuity and strength of the oral traditions of Ireland. In this excellent book, itself a skilful blend of social history and folk traditions, Dr O'Dowd has produced a notable addition to the ethnological literature available in Britain.

ALEXANDER FENTON

THE PURITAN–PROVINCIAL VISION

Scottish and American Literature in the Nineteenth Century

Susan Manning

Cambridge University Press, Cambridge (1990)

241 pp. £32.50 ISBN 0 521 37237 2

This is not an easy book to read, but it is a work of much labour and thought, and it presents a unique perspective by linking Scottish and American literature—in contrast to that of metropolitan England—in the nineteenth century. Susan Manning is very careful to state in her preface 'that this is an essay in literary criticism, not literary history, the history of ideas or a comparative study of influences'. She is concerned, she writes, 'with a particular use of language and with the literary consequences of the assumptions that lie behind it'.

To this end Manning devotes her first chapter to 'Calvin's theology and the puritan mind', which includes an examination of one opponent of the puritans in England, John Selden, and his charge that while an Anglican could cheerfully concede that 'disputes in religion will never be ended', Calvinists, in Manning's words, 'demanded resolution', though the very nature of Calvinist thought made this difficult if not impossible. Manning writes that 'the Calvinist is unable to imagine the 'other' as anything but a message to him, and distorted reflection of something within' (p. 15), thus 'otherness was a threat unless it could be colonised for the self'. In other words, the aggressive interrogation of the morality of others characteristic of Calvinists originated in the fear of error and sin central to the relationship the Calvinist adopted towards the Deity.

Manning develops her work on Calvinism by original and demanding readings of writers such as Emerson, Fenimore Cooper, Edgar Allan Poe, Melville and Hawthorne in America, and Sir Walter Scott, James Hogg, John Galt and Thomas Carlyle in Scotland. Her chapters entitled 'the pursuit of the double' and 'spectators, spies and spectres: the observer's stance' develop her interpretation of Calvinist-influenced language in 'puritan–provincial' literature of the nineteenth century, unable 'to know the hidden truth' yet driven by desire to seek it.

This book deserves high praise for building on recent interest in links between Scottish and American culture in a unique manner that brings fresh insights to the literature of both countries. A short review cannot do full justice to its complexities, but it can at least draw attention to the originality and interest of its approach.

ALEX MURDOCH

STRANGERS WITHIN THE REALM

Cultural Margins of the First British Empire

Eds. Bernard Bailyn and Philip D. Morgan

University of North Carolina Press: Chapel Hill (1991)

456 pp. $39.95 (cloth) ISBN 0 8078 1952 2 and $14.95 (paper) ISBN 0 8078 4311 3

This collection of essays deserves wider circulation in Britain than that usually achieved by books published by the University of North Carolina Press. The volume has grown from a conference held at Williamsburg, Virginia in 1985 on 'The Social World of Britain and America, 1600–1820'. After the death of the initiator of the project, Stephen Botein, Bernard Bailyn and Philip Morgan have carried it to triumphant conclusion. While English historians have become more insular in recent decades,work on the history of former elements of the British empires has become focused on the national aspects of subsequent development. 'It seems doubtful, for example, ' the editors write in their introduction, 'that historians of British Canada regularly read histories of the British West Indies.' Implicit in this argument is the point that, despite some noteworthy recent exceptions, historians of Ireland, Scotland and America do not read each others' histories either. This book, presented by the editors as 'transnational in spirit, pluralist and multicultural in approach', should help promote a more comparative study of the various elements of the first British Empire. As such it follows in the pioneering tradition established by Angus Calder in 1981, with the publication of his *Revolutionary Empire: The Rise of the English-speaking Empires from the Fifteenth Century to the 1780s.*

The list of contributors is impressive, including Nicholas Canny on Ireland, Eric Richards on Scotland, James Merrell on Indians and Colonists in America, Philip Morgan on Africans and African-Americans, A. G. Roeber on the Germans in America, Maldwyn Jones on the 'Scotch-Irish', Michael Craton on the West Indies, J. M. Bumsted on Canada and a concluding essay by Jacob M. Price on the impact of the American colonies on the economies and societies of Scotland and England. All collections of essays are something of a mixed bag, but this is a strong collection, well produced, with an extensive index.

Naturally, a review appearing in a Scottish journal must devote attention to Eric Richards' essay, 'Scotland and the Uses of the Atlantic Empire', which offers a wide-ranging view of Scotland and its relations with both England and America throughout the eighteenth century. In this he is able to draw on his own work on the history of the Scottish Highlands while integrating it with much of the large amount of scholarship on eighteenth-century Scotland which has appeared over the past twenty years. He uses Nicholas Phillipson's work on Scotland as a cultural province, and T. C. Smout's work on the Scottish economy, to contrast the varying fortunes of Highland and Lowland Scotland in the eighteenth century. The essay at points reads as if it had been little revised since 1985, as there are few references to publications after that date, but though this might affect some minor points, it does not reduce the general value of Richards' piece. It attempts to integrate Highland and Lowland Scottish history, and take account of intellectual, social, economic and political perspectives, so that just as the book aspires to break down barriers between national histories, so Richards tries to break down barriers that have operated in the writing of Scottish history, using his unique perspective as a Scottish historian based in Australia.

Hopefully, it will not just be Scottish historians who read Richards' essay. *Strangers Within the Realm* offers a unique opportunity to gain access to overviews of parallel historiographies, and further a comparative understanding of eighteenth-century Scotland in a much broader social and economic context. The appearance of a paperback edition is particularly welcome.

ALEX MURDOCH

RECENT JOURNALS

Scottish Studies Vol. 30 (1991). The Journal of the School of Scottish Studies, 27 George Square, Edinburgh EH8 9LD.

John Bannerman, The Clarsach and the Clarsair
William Gillies, Gaelic Songs of the 'Forty-Five
Donald E. Meek, Dugald Sinclair: The Life and Work of a Highland Itinerant Missionary
John Shaw, 'Sgeulachd a' Chait Bhig 's a' Chait Mhoir': A Gaelic Variant of 'The Two Travellers' (AT 613).

Tocher. Tales, Songs, Tradition, No. 44 (1992). Selected from the Archives of the School of Scottish Studies, 27 George Square, Edinburgh EH8 9LD.

Willie MacPhee—Last of the Travelling Tinsmiths
Burning the Clavie at Burghead
Rannan Bréige (Lying Verses)
Blàr Thràigh Ghruinneart (The Battle of Tràigh Ghruinneart)
William and Norah Montgomerie
The Broonie
Folk cures

Northern Scotland, Vol. 12 (1992), The Journal of the Centre for Scottish Studies, University of Aberdeen, King's College, Old Aberdeen AB9 2UB.

E. D. P. Torrie, The early urban site of New Aberdeen: a reappraisal of the evidence
David Ditchburn, The pirate, the policeman and the pantomine star: Aberdeen's alternative economy in the early fifteenth century
Albert Bil, The formation of new settlements in the Perthshire Highlands, 1660–1780

Richard J. Smith, Shetland and the Greenland whaling industry, 1780–1872
Alastair J. Durie, Tourism and commercial photography in Victorian Scotland: the rise and fall of G. W. Wilson & Co, 1852–1908
Malcolm D. Prentis, From Aberdeen to Coburg: a lad o' pairts in Australia
J. R. Coull, The development of the fishery districts of Scotland

Scottish Economic and Social History, Vol.11 (1991). The Journal of the Economic and Social History Society of Scotland, c/o Department of Economic and Social History, Edinburgh University, 50 George Square, Edinburgh EH8 9JY.
T. M. Devine and *B. Harnesk*, The Decline of Farm Service: A Comparative Study of Scotland and Sweden
Cynthia M. Atherton, The Development of the Middle Class Suburb: The West End of Glasgow
S. McKinstry, The Albion Motor Car Company: Growth and Specialisation 1899–1918
Callum G. Brown, Similarisation: A Theory in Danger

Ulster Folklife Vol.38 (1992), Ulster Folk and Transport Museum, Cultra, Holywood, Co. Down, Northern Ireland.
Valerie Hall, The Woodlands of the Lower Bann Valley in the Seventeenth Century: The Documentary Evidence
Fionnula Nic Suibhne, 'On the Straw' and Other Aspects of Pregnancy and Childbirth from the Oral Tradition of Women in Ulster
Charles G. Ludlow, an Eighteenth Century Irish Saltworks as Described in the Castleward Papers
Dermot Francis, Derry and the 1916 Rising
Nora Bates, Growing up in Saintfield, Co.Down
Gerard Downey and *Gerard Stockman*, The Doctor and Death: A Gaelic Folktale from Tyrone
Vivienne Pollock, Systems of Boat Ownership in the Co. Down Fishing Fleet
Linda-May Ballard, Some Aspects of Tradition among Female Religious in Ulster
A. J. Hughes, Deirdre Flanagan's 'Belfast and the Place-Names Therein', in Translation
Karen Corrigan, Glens Dialect from Moira O'Neill to Michael J. Murphy

Folk Life. Journal of Ethnological Studies, Vol 30 (1991–92), c/o Museum of English Rural Life, University of Reading, Whiteknights, PO Box 229, Reading RG6 2AG
Christine Faulkner, Hops and Hop Pickers of the Midlands
Alan Harris, Gorse in the East Riding of Yorkshire
Eldbjørg Fossgard, Farming Women and Technology
Jill Batts, The Devon Splint Basket
Emmanuel Cooper, The People's Art
David Goa, The Seasons of Celebration Project
Caroline Macafee, Acumsinery: Is it Too Late To Collect Traditional Dialect?
Nigel Wright, Naughty But Nice?
Beth Thomas, Here Today, Gone Tomorrow? Language and Dialect in a Welsh community

Rural History, Economy, Society, Culture, vol. 3, No. 2 (1992), Cambridge University Press, The Edinburgh Building, Shaftesbury Road, Cambridge CB2 2RU.
David Postles, Brewing and the Peasant Economy: some Manors in Late Medieval Devon
K. D. M. Snell, Settlement, Poor law and the Rural Historian: New Approaches and Opportunities
Robert A. Dodgshon, Farming Practice in the Western Highlands and Irelands before Crofting: A Study in Cultural Inertia or Opportunity Costs?
Ulf Jonsson, The Paradox of Share Tenancy under Capitalism: A Comparative Perspective on late Nineteenth- and Twentieth-Century French and Italian Sharecropping
Mark B. Lapping, American Rural Planning, Development Policy and the Centrality of the Federal State: An Interpretative History

Ethnologia Europea Centralis Vol. 1 (1992), Dr Jana Volfová, Regio Publsihers, Úvoz 4, 602 00 Brno, Czechoslovakia.
Vaclav Frolec, Cultural Space of Central and South eastern Europe: Dimension of Folk Culture
Soňa Švecová, Ethnographic Groups and Regions in Slovakia
Josef Vařeka, Alena Plessingerová: Directions, Results and Purposes of Research in Traditional Building Culture in Czech Villages
Vaclav Frolec, Wedding Ceremony under Change. Situation in Czech Lands

This new initiative from Czechoslovakia is greatly to be welcomed. The periodical 'concentrates on ethno-cultural processes, cultural identity and national minorities as well as on cultural and scientific cooperation in Europe. It aims at becoming a scientific informational link between the countries of former East Europe and the rest of Europe, USA and Canada'. It is an independent periodical, and so will be dependent on support from fellow-institutions. Subscriptions, including postage, are 15 US dollars; it is available at the address above.